A Life
Less Ordinary

JULIA BRUNO

First edition January 2021

Cover design by S J Bekta
Typesetting by M J Prowse

Dedication

This book is dedicated to those people who are curious about life's *whys*? It is for those who feel that life has been working against them at times, for those who wonder what is out there in the Universe, for those who are on a journey of personal or spiritual growth and for those who want to move forward.

Sometimes you have to get past the uncomfortable, the unbearable and the unthinkable to find the reasons behind it all.

I wrote this book for you. There is a reason you have chosen to be here on this page. I hope this book leaves you with questions, and you go on your journey to find the answers.

Happy travels through this beautiful life.

LOVE always,
Julia

,

Mum

And now she's gone, my bestest friend,
No mum to love me till the end,
No phone to ring,
No song to sing.

No smile so bright,
No heart so warm,
No kiss goodnight,
My heart is torn.

But all's not lost, she still is there,
She's in the rocking of the chair,
The leaves that rustle in the trees,
The warm and sunny, balmy breeze,
The buzz the flutter of the bees,
The wave and ripple of the seas.

She's in my heart, my mind, my soul,
She gave me life, she gave me goals,
She'll always be right next to me,
No matter what, right there she'll be.

To wander with me through my days,
To guide me, show me all the ways,
To live my life as full can be,
Till this life too is done with me.

Julia Bruno

Chapter One

Sometimes it feels like I am stuck at the top of a tower…no lift…no stairs…no door…just windows all around, looking down on the world, everyone going about their business. I can see them…hear them…feel the busy beat of life, and still taste it. I remember the hunger for the excitement of it all; I had not always been stuck in the tower. Things started very differently for me.

If my little hand had known how, it would have written, *Dear diary, I tried so hard to stop my dad from hurting my mum today. I saw what he was doing, and something came over me. I beat my tiny fists on his leg, crying and begging him to stop hurting my mummy. He pushed me away so hard I flew through the air and hit my back full force against the corner of the television. I was so upset that my tummy was really hurting.* I have wondered over the years if it was because of this day and the blow to my tiny back that my left kidney stopped growing.

I had been told and shown countless times of the way he dug his knuckles into the corners of her eyes and twisted hard, leaving them black and blue. But she didn't need to tell me; I already knew. I was standing there watching. They treated me as if I was a vase or a chair, with no feelings, but I saw and heard everything.

He was young and drunk and took his lessons from his own violent father. 'Learned behaviour' I think they call it. He later told me he was with my mum because she was the popular girl about town, with a good job and a family business. It was a step up in the world for a bin man's son.

He was a very stubborn and vain man, my dad, who styled himself on the Bee Gee's singer Barry Gibb. He crashed his car more than once by looking longingly in the rearview mirror at himself. My mum had had enough one day; she found out he was cheating on her.

His younger brother, feeling sorry for Mum, told her where Ian was and who with. That was the final straw. With all her fingernails embedded in his back, she found the strength to throw him out. "He is never coming back," she said. My tummy ached for years.

Once she found that strength, she clung on to it for a while. She was a beautiful, kind, caring and selfless human being, my mum, with a smile that could defrost a freezer at a glance. Back in those days, you would not want to cross my mum.

I remember how bad my tummy had been after Ian had left, I was four years old, and I constantly strained and found it very hard to go to the toilet. There were just a lot of confused messages between my tummy and my bottom, and it sometimes left a little mess in my undies.

At nursery, the teacher found out and punished me by not letting me join in sports day with the other kids. I sat alone in the classroom, until my mum came and asked where I was. That day she strung the teacher up against the wall by her neck and threatened her for daring to punish me for something out of my control. Yay, go Colleen! She was amazing!

There was a year of happiness, with just Mum, baby Lindsay and me. Mum would sing Cliff Richard's 'Living Doll' to me. She said I was her little doll. We were so happy in those days. She worked driving Grandad's mobile shops, which were big heavy vans laden with all sorts of goodies and no power steering; something she said accounted for her strong back and shoulders.

Nan looked after us children whilst Mum was at work. She was fabulous, my nan, and she loved to put on her airs and graces. She told me her name was Dorothea Juliana, like some bygone silent film star, and that I was named after her. She played the piano and taught me to exercise every day. She loved warming her legs by the fire (the unheated house was ice cold), setting fire to her skirts many times as they dangled over the flames. She loved to put on her posh voice but cursed something rotten at my grandad and anyone else she didn't like. There was a fag constantly hanging from the side of her ruby red, lipsticked lips, dropping ash into the egg butty she would make for the bread man, milkman, pop man or any other deliveryman.

She was kindness served with a slice of bitterness, my nan, who turned out just to be plain old Doris Julia. I didn't find that out until she died. I guess she spent a lot of her life dreaming of being Dorothea and being bitter at my grandad for taking her away from her home town of Norwich with the promise of the good life. All she got was a lifetime in a council house and £5 a week to feed five of them. I don't think she ever forgave him. After all, she had been an independent woman when she met him, selling her own house to fund his little enterprise of three mobile shops and a petrol station/garage.

He was well known around Scarborough, my grandad, as much for his tightness as his shops. From an early age, I was taught to weigh potatoes into 5lb bags and how to choose different sized ones so the bags didn't go overweight. For my trouble, my mum would give me slices of the best luncheon meat and plastic-looking cheese that came in a big long block. My grandad, if alone, would give me nothing.

I remember one day packing and stacking with Georgina (my four-years-older cousin) and sitting, clinging on the shop counter on the way home, facing the penny sweets. I thought we deserved one, so I reached over and picked an Anglo Bubbly. We shared it as they were big, and he would have seen it in our mouths if we had one each. I thought I was being clever. I had no idea he was looking in the rearview mirror. I didn't do it again!

I loved my grandad, James Noel (known to everyone as Noel) very much, and spent hours with him as he retired and took to his garden to escape my nan. He taught me about his different crops and how to grow them. He had amazing green fingers and made his own greenhouses out of old wood-framed windows.

I was the only one of the grandchildren to spend time with him. We would sit and watch the snooker or horse racing, cuddled up. He never cuddled anyone else, including my nan. I always kissed him hello and goodbye, and every single time for my whole life, he blew his cheek out and made a raspberry sound. My name for him was Grand, and he loved it. I was close to both my nan and grandad. I miss them very much.

I have sensed my nan many times, mostly before my mum passed away. I would get a whiff of *Tweed* perfume, and I would know she was there. It happened to me once in the middle of the supermarket, and an overwhelming sense of 'be on guard', so my bag never left my side, and I hurried along, ditched my trolley, and left as quickly as possible.

I am sure that many times my nan and my mum, working from the spirit world, have saved me in one form or another.

Life was great for a whole year or so in our little council house, until Mum decided to answer an advert in the personals. How she found him, I will never know. His name was Peter, and his hometown was Portsmouth.

He worked for Lockheed Aircraft in Saudi Arabia and was a clerk, I believe. He seemed nice enough, although even as a little girl, I felt something was not quite right when I was around him. However, he was kind enough to my brother and me, and Mum seemed to like him. Later, my mum told me she married the first time because she was in love with a good-looking man, and she wasn't going to marry another one.

In the end, her theory that only good-looking men cheated turned out to be seriously flawed! He bowled her over with meals out and a nice weekend at Langley Castle with my brother and me. The memory is of the small square castle where we were babysat by a lady on the end of the telephone while Mum and Peter dined. The photograph in the grounds with my little brother has always been a favourite of mine. Goodness knows why she chose to dress us in matching green and navy terry-towelling tracksuits. We were neither twins, nor the same age. Luckily, my long baby blond hair still gave away that I was a girl. She had weird fads, my mum, and I think that was just one of them.

I would never have believed at that time that one day I would end up calling the Langley Castle Estate my home for a while, in a cottage nestled in the woods opposite the castle.

Within a year, we had moved to Portsmouth and Mum and Peter married.

I don't remember the event, but I do remember the photo. Mum always had the most incredible backcombed hair, and she never went anywhere without this massive extension of hair on her head, a tribute to her youth in the '60s. It was copied by a few, but she was the master of the backcomb! When 'curly' came into fashion in the '80s, she combined it with another one of her bright ideas. She wore what would be described now as an afro. I think she may have been single-handedly responsible for the hole in the ozone layer, the amount of hairspray it took to keep that thing out! It was so tall that her passport said she was 5ft 10 (they daren't flatten her hair when measuring her). She was, in fact, several inches shorter, although she maintained that she was 5ft 10 for many years after. In all the sixty years of her life, she was always impeccable –slightly out of date but always beautiful, smart and wearing the biggest smile you have ever seen. She shone from the inside out, my mum. Men could see that too, however.

She became pregnant with my baby brother Richard, very quickly after the wedding, whilst I was enrolled into my worst nightmare.

I can't tell you the name of the school. I must have chosen to forget it, along with everything else from those darkest of days. I don't know how it started, but my tummy was worse than ever. Mum had this new man, new baby, new house and new life and I had felt pushed aside a little, I guess. Feeling constantly uncomfortable, I knew something wasn't right. I was just a tiny little blonde doll of a six-year-old girl. I should have been happy and full of confidence.

I am unsure which came first, the bullies or the marks in my pants. Either way, one led to the other, which led back again in a vicious circle. How they knew or why they did it, I have no clue. All details I chose to forget. Two older girls at school took it upon themselves to check my undies every day for marks. I was pushed into the toilets, backed into a cubicle and forced to pull my undies down. My pants were inspected (marks were unavoidable in my constant state of straining. Unable to go to the toilet, it led to skid marks, and now on top of that, the fear of what I was going through just made it more impossible to poop).

I stood emotionless and cold. I couldn't even look because I knew. The knot in my stomach grew by the day. This was my routine every lunchtime. Every single day I was punished. I knew I would be taken to the corner of the schoolyard like a condemned man.

I didn't need to be dragged. I knew I had to go. The fear and the dread are still there in me deep down.

As I write this, I can feel it. Maybe a little bit of that hell still lives there inside me, pushed down to the deepest depths. It always happened under the coats that were usually thrown there by kids running around getting hot, playing tag and kiss chase. If not, it was the girl's coats and mine. In that corner out of sight, my skirt was lifted, undies pulled down, and the two girls touched me in my private area, penetrating and hurting me with their fingers, pulling and tearing. Putting their hands up my shirt, grabbing and squeezing at my chest. I sat every day, unable to speak, frozen, cold and dead inside. They made me thank them for my punishment. I knew it was wrong; it felt so shameful, so bad, so evil. But I hated myself, and I blamed myself. After all, it was my fault there were marks.

Every day the thought of going to school filled me with terror. My blood ran cold, knowing exactly what I was walking into. I could not tell anyone as I had been threatened with even worse if I were to tell.

Who would believe me? I was shy and timid and wouldn't say boo to a goose. I couldn't even look people in the eye. I knew that they would know about me if I did, they would be able to read me. I already thought everyone knew what was inside of me — everyone knew I was dirty. I felt completely alone in the world. I walked around every day with shame and hoped I would just die, because nobody except those girls would notice if I just didn't turn up anymore. How come I ended up there in that school? Why me? What had I done? I was a very good little girl. I despised Peter for making us move there.

I realise now that those girls had to have been going through their own nightmare, to know how to use sexual places as a punishment. That's what they must have thought was happening to them in their own lives. I think the girls were sisters. My tummy got so bad that I ended up being force-fed bran rings the size of bangles and as hard as the fake dog pooh they looked like. I was taken from doctor to doctor, ultimately being explored internally by a consultant with very big hands. I had to bend down on all fours on the hospital bed, in front of not only my mum, but my sadistic stepdad and his even more sadistic mother. They all watched, and I was just glad I could not see their faces. I can still see the picture of the sterile white room as if I had left my body and was watching it all, seeing and feeling the humiliation. Nobody thought to find out that the problem was not in my bottom but in my soul, having witnessed so much as a tiny girl, and then having been sent to the school from hell.

As I began writing this book, I found it very difficult to bring out all of these memories again, but knew I had to. I have never been back to Portsmouth and wouldn't want to go. I find even saying the word chokes me. I have even found it very difficult to bring into my own mind the name of the estate in which we lived. I re-read the beginning as I wrote it and decided I would try and find out the name of the school. As I typed out the name of the estate reluctantly, my stomach knotted once more. I looked at what was on the screen, and Wikipedia caught my eye, I was hesitant to read anything but felt compelled.

What I read shook me to my core. In the year 2000 residents of this estate rioted. They had compiled a list of paedophiles – some convicted, some suspected and some named by women who had been abused themselves. A group of vigilantes had torched cars, attacked people and drove some of them out from their homes. I was blown away. I cried from deep inside for a minute or so before the tears even came. This had been an area where child sexual abuse had been prevalent. I read a story of a few women who said they had been abused there when they were younger. I wondered as I read, was it her? Or her? I cried, thinking it was once again my fault. Had I spoken up as a six-year-old, maybe my story would have been investigated, then their story may have come to light.

But it was not my fault. I was six. I will never know the names of those girls who abused me. I will never have my day in court. My vindication will come from writing my story, allowing the pain to be etched onto these pages hopefully, instead of all the years it has been etched into my soul. In many ways, my childhood innocence ended there. I became harder inside. I could feel it. Still extremely shy and sweet, these experiences had taught me how to cope when times were tough, how to die inside and still carry on. Already by six years old, I had had enough life experiences to toughen me up.

As luck would have it, Peter could not handle home life very well and soon went back to work in Saudi Arabia, leaving Mum to look after us alone. She refused to stay in Portsmouth as she had never liked it. Instead, thankfully she moved us all back to Scarborough where we belonged, to a beautiful little semi on a new estate. That is when I met Lorraine, my next-door neighbour.

I was wary of girls. They were horrible. Still to this day, I don't like the company of more than one girl at a time. Lou soon taught me how to trust again. She was so kind, sweet, loving and generous to a fault, so unassuming. In her thick-rimmed NHS glasses and her hand-knit clothes, she let me in and shared everything with me. We became instant best friends.

She had her share of troubles too, having been born with curvature of the spine and terrible eyesight. Although, she was a hit in the primary school yard, often playing kiss chase with the boys, having two boyfriends at once, twins called Stevie and Glen Griffiths.

While I, on the other hand, was painfully shy. I blended in with the walls, unseen, unheard, with a secret crush on a boy in a blue cagoule called Guy, who never knew I existed. It more or less stayed like that with boys right up until the last year of Pindar Secondary school, except for one poor boy who had the misfortune to have been born with a Brillo pad for hair. He professed his adoration for me in the schoolyard, so I agreed to go out with him. I felt I owed him because he liked me, although I didn't like him but rather felt sorry for him. We walked home from school holding hands. I felt so embarrassed that it was over by the time we got to my door. Poor Adam, the first heart I broke.

Anyway, back to being seven, eight years old. Living in a new house on a new street had its advantages, as we had a whole builder's yard to play in. Long before the days of CCTV and security, roof trusses became dens. Half-built houses were great for hide and seek or playing families, and partition board was the best pavement chalk. We had an abundance of nails, screws, bits of wood offcuts, and bits of bricks. However dangerous it was, we knew how to go out and play!

There were no computer games at that time. Instead, we would cycle for miles, right up to the beach at Cayton Bay, having a sneaky look around the caravan sites, pretending we were holidaymakers.

It was all very innocent. We were little adventurers exploring the world, until that is, we got a little wake-up call. In the house that the Pascoe's eventually moved into across the street, Lou, my cousin Georgina and I were having a 'nosey' and went to look upstairs in the house, giggling and laughing as always. Suddenly a figure jumped out from behind a door, and we all screamed, scrambling as fast as we could to the stairs and trying not to fall down. I turned to look back and saw Georgina still at the top, a big figure of a man behind her, his hands cupping her breasts (she was four years older than I was, and had developed some little boobs by this time). The look in her eyes was of sheer terror. I did not know what to do but shouted for my mum as I ran out of the building. Luckily, Georgina was just a few seconds behind. He knew he would have been caught, so let her go.

We were so frightened but dared not say anything to anyone, as we should not have been in the house. The 'dirty electrician', as we aptly named him, became a figure I was very scared of, darting into bushes and over walls if I saw his car coming towards me around the village. The odd time I saw him by mistake he would make lewd faces, making me all the more nervous, I felt he was capable of something horrible.

Chapter Two

By the time I reached the age of ten, we had set
off on an adventure. Sick of six weeks marriage a
year, Mum decided with Peter that we should
spend two years in Saudi Arabia. The first time
any of us had left the country, let alone flown.
Mum was travelling alone with three kids, ten
and under! Relocating to the other side of the
world, as she called it. We got a taxi from Nan
and Grandad's house down to Heathrow, with a
driver friend of my family called George North.
He was bald like Telly Savalas, with a Burt
Reynolds moustache and a heavy smell of
tobacco, but a smile that made me feel safe on
that big car journey. It felt as if we were driving
to the end of the Earth.

At Heathrow, a Boeing 747 was waiting
to take us off into the sunset. Wow! I fell in love
that day. The magic of aviation hit me with a
love I still have today. Thirty-eight years and
hundreds of flights later (although to my
disappointment, I have never flown again in
another 747 yet). I looked down at the clouds
and thought it was heaven because in those
clouds, I saw people's faces; they were all lined
up, as if they were in beds in a row. My nose
was glued to the window for the whole flight, as
it usually still is today. I was allowed to go up
into the cockpit and talk to the pilots, of which

there were three, and the most amazing array of buttons and dials. I was so awestruck that I didn't even lift my head to look out of the cockpit window. We stopped in Jeddah to let some people off, so got to land and take off again. It wasn't long before the plane doors opened in Riyadh. I stepped out into what can only be described as a baking hot oven. It felt all-embracing as it surrounded me and almost took my breath away.

Saudi it turned out was not as Mum had expected. She had never been further than Aviemore in Scotland for a holiday, and the culture difference was a shock to her. As a lifelong insomniac, not permitted to take her sleeping tablets with her, she was a walking zombie half the time. Having to cover up neck to ankle to wrist, I wore light coloured long sleeve dresses, which I am sure were for boys, as my brothers wore the same. We had to walk behind the men, which tickled my brothers. It was a wonderful sight of fairy-tale princes' palaces, with big rubbish dumps, or shacks next to them. Many people lived under date trees at the side of the road, selling the produce as it grew. Defecating at the side of the road was a common sight in those days. They weren't even embarrassed as they lifted their dresses up and crouched down in full view of everyone. There were no women drivers, but boys as young as I was, ten years old, driving big jeep-type vehicles. There was a magic, though, that surged through my veins, of being only ten in a place so far removed from all that I had known.

The gold souks, brimming with everything you could think of made from gold. Nearby was Chop Square, a real deterrent if ever there were one. Limbs and the like chopped off in a public arena as punishment! I was glad I didn't get to watch, although my middle brother wanted to go. The streets were filled with smells of huge slabs of meat cooking on spits, although we were never permitted to try it. Peter said they were camels' legs. The shape seemed to fit, which put us off anyway.

I learned to love the magnificence of midnight shopping. This was the coolest part of the day and with fewer prayer stops. I still love it to this day. This was a time where shops in the UK closed at five pm weekdays, half-day on Wednesdays and all day Sunday. The supermarkets were stocked full of not only Arabic produce but also American goodies. Most foreigners, including us, lived on American compounds, secure from the outside world. I fell in love with all things American, from Richie Rich, and Sports Billy cartoons, to the copious amounts of Kool-Aid, Twinkies and Popsicles we were allowed to have. I revisited my love of all things American recently, as we can now get those little treats in the UK. Once I excitedly purchased a Twinkie with fond memories of a sweet cake filled with delicious cream, only to find it was actually a washing sponge filled with Crisco type sweetened lard. What was I thinking?

The best thing ever though, was Herfy Bar, the Arabian equivalent of a McDonald's, something we did not have back home in Scarborough. With skinny fries, large cokes or root beer and a bread bun stacked to the sky with wafer-thin beef, it was heaven. We weren't allowed our own bun (we could only have fries), but my mum always shared hers. We would sit around her like three chirping chicks, all trying to get a slice of her beef. I got ten riyals pocket money (two pounds at that time), and I liked to save it so that if we visited Herfy Bar, I could sit on my own table with my own 'stacked to the sky' beef sandwich. My brothers looked on with envy and drooling, after wasting their pocket money on sweets, but I savoured every morsel, and shared none! It was mine, bought with my own money.

Saudi represented a fun, mind-expanding period. School was going to break up soon for three months, so we didn't get enrolled. It was an endless round of sunshine, swimming and Popsicles. Maybe it was not so much fun for my little brother Ricky, who was four at the time. Unable to swim, he had his armbands on.

Always the enterprising person I am today, I saw an idea of how to keep him afloat, and the light bulb went on in my head. If he put them on his feet, he would be able to walk on water! I then convinced Lindsay that such a feat was possible. Ricky believed us and sat on the edge while we put the armbands on his ankles, telling him to hold himself up straight and walk fast. The first attempt was a disaster. He immediately sank, feet still in the air, unable to right himself, as he could not stop his feet floating upwards. Luckily, Mum saw what was happening and shimmied over in her rubber ring.

Always terrified of water, she couldn't swim. It put the fear of the gods into her, but her huge tractor-tyre sized rubber ring helped her negotiate the water. He was OK and upright again. After a brief telling off, Mum paddled back to where she was sunning herself on the water.

I told my little brother off, as clearly he didn't move fast enough. I figured if he was quicker, he would stay upright. Still determined, I put the armbands back on his feet, and he stepped into the water again, "Run quickly this time!" I said. Well, we all know the result of that experiment! We didn't get to play anymore that day. My punishment was to give Rick one of my flip-flops, as one of his got stuck into some sinking mud on the way home. Are you kidding?

I was expected to hop all the way home? The streets were hot enough to fry an egg on, my mum used to say, so I fashioned my paper drinks cup into a toe cover to protect them from the heat. My brother and I laughed for many years, recalling that story.

Another adventure was to go diamond picking in the desert, getting up before dawn in an effort to see the desert diamonds glisten as the sun rose. We took a picnic with boiled eggs and bananas, and had to wee behind a cactus, as there wasn't a toilet for hundreds of miles. As it turned out, the desert took longer to get to than was thought, and we missed the sunrise, but it was a great expedition all the same. All those days were an adventure, an amazing way to spend a part of your childhood.

I learned to love the call to prayers, something that was echoed and brought memories flooding back years later when I bought my little house In Turkey. It sounds so beautiful to me that I could close my eyes and be instantly ten years old again. I sat so many times on my terrace in the sunshine there, with my eyes closed listening to the sound of the mosques in the distance.

We were enrolled in school, Riyadh International or 'RICS', after the summer holidays had finished. It was quite a long drive there, and I remember being very nervous on that first day, boarding the yellow American school bus. Armed with school bag and packed lunch, I felt like I was going on a real adventure. RICS was just like any other school, an endless round of lessons intersected by lunchtime with what was now a very warm packed lunch. The only interesting subject I can remember was Arabic. I only ended up having two lessons but can still count to seven and say 'thank you' thirty-eight years later, which is useful only up until I want to buy eight of something! After being at school only two weeks, everything changed. The government decided not to renew seven-year-old Lindsay's visa, so we were taken out of school. Soon Mum and us kids headed back home to Scarborough, this time on a Tri-Star.

Chapter Three

Lou and I picked up where we had left off, firmly glued together. The next couple of years were full of the usual girl's stuff, playing outside, talking about boys, experimenting with hair and makeup and trying to make our very unfashionable clothes look OK. Friday nights were shopping nights for Maureen and Bryan, her mum and dad. Lou always had a Vesta curry for her tea on a Friday. I thought this very exotic. We never got anything foreign, even in Saudi we ate as English as possible. Ours was definitely a 'meat and potatoes' house.

Lou also taught me how to make garlic toast with butter and garlic salt as we had never even had pasta or pizza before, until McCain's started to make basic pizza and my uncle John brought some home for us to try. Pasta was tinned spaghetti bolognese on toast, real pasta I did not try till I was about 18!

At school, I was as painfully shy as ever. My cousin Georgina was in her final year, and I sat with her some of the time. She had a secret love for the hottest guy in school, Heath! Wow, he was a dreamboat, with ash-blond hair worn Simon le Bon style, chiselled cheekbones and jawline, and a furrowed brow. (I found out later I had a liking for the Neanderthal brow, Matt, my future husband, having a very strong one himself).

I too had a massive crush on Heath. Georgina never dared tell him to his face about her love for him but wrote him letters, sent him tapes and presents. Heath thought they were from somebody else, a rotund girl with long ginger hair, so, when Georgina asked him round for tea, he somehow went to the ginger girl's house. He thought it was funny. Sitting with Georgina and her friend Sue one day, Heath came wandering by. "Heath, my little cousin has a crush on you", she shouted. OMG, I wanted the ground to open up and swallow me. He sat next to me and put his arm round me, and I went the colour of beetroot. She thought it was hilarious. One day when I was nineteen, I would get my own back on her, big style, as he became mine for a short while, and I had great pleasure telling her.

It was about this time I found out about my kidneys. One night my friend Lou and her mum were over at our house. Lou and I had been playing, chatting and doing girls stuff in my room. This was a bit of a luxury as Mum rarely let anyone in the house. She was funny like that, but I guess if she let Lou in, she couldn't say no to my brothers and before you knew it, there would be a riot of kids. I must have been in pain --I don't recall -- but I walked in the living room with Lou right behind me and collapsed onto the floor. An ambulance was called, and I remember waking on a children's ward in the hospital. Mum explained that they had found out I had pyelonephritis (where the valve going from the kidney to the bladder is faulty and splashes urine back up, causing infection). My left kidney was seriously underdeveloped. This wasn't the best news, but I was really more concerned about when I was going to eat. I was starving! Eventually the food trolley came through, and everyone got their little tray with a plate covered with an opaque coloured cloche. Oh, my goodness, hot sausage roll, chips and beans. It smelled amazing. It felt like I had not eaten in a week. I sat upright to tuck in when a nurse quickly shouted, "No, she is nil by mouth" and quickly swiped it from under my nose. I don't remember when or what it was that I ate next, but that meal will always be the one that got away. The smell of a hot sausage roll always makes me think of that day. I don't think I have ever eaten that combo since, maybe in a silent protest.

The one great thing about being diagnosed with chronic kidney disease as a teenager is that the doctors told me I had to drink as much clear liquid as possible (including lemonade). From that day onward, I was allowed to go to the school office whenever I wanted, to get a drink. I only ever did this in Mr Reese's class because he would always let me. I would happily skive off, skip down the corridor, have a big glug of lemonade, and skip back, thinking I was some special case.

The novelty didn't last that long though. I got sick of having to lug two-litre bottles of lemonade a mile to school. I wasn't easy to carry in my '80s plastic open-weaved school bag.

I think it was around this time that I noticed things were going a bit wrong for Mum. Peter only came back for six weeks a year (thank God), but they would often be in the kitchen with the door closed, arguing, as if the closed kitchen door would have stopped me from hearing them, or from knowing it was me they were arguing about. He controlled everything when he was home. There was no give and take. It was often about my bedtime. Mum, being on her own at night, let me stay up and watch things like Dallas and Dynasty.

I remember Mum saying her first husband was physically abusive, and the second was emotionally abusive. She said she would rather have had a smack in the face anytime, as she knew where she was with that. Someone as soft as my mum was far too open and vulnerable to mental cruelty, as she called it. This was not the last time she would meet a cruel man.

Peter often fancied a Chinese takeaway while he was at home, and would suggest this by asking Mum if she was peckish. Occasionally one or more of us would overhear and pipe up, "I'm peckish too." My brothers weren't so keen, but I loved Chinese food once introduced to it. It is still my favourite today. I remember much more than once being excited by the talk of Chinese, only to hear Peter say to Mum that he wanted an easy night with no kids around. Really? You have no kids around the other forty-six weeks of the year! I was never any bother. My chair was pulled right up to and under the TV cabinet. They couldn't even see me, but I remember having to have an early night again, and listening to the sounds as the takeaway was brought in, the smells drifting up to my room, making my tummy growl like there was a lion loose in there. If she could, Mum would sneak a sweet and sour pork ball up for me, on her way for a fake toilet visit. I knew she felt guilty that it was made to seem that we kids were just an inconvenience. He did no parenting anyway, but was very keen to lay down his rules. I always played outside until about nine pm in the summer as Mum was quite laid back. I was in bed for nine-thirty to ten. When Peter was home, I wasn't allowed out after tea, and I was in bed by eight pm, a very early time for a twelve to thirteen-year-old.

It was great for the rest of the year, though. I was Mum's companion and confidante when he wasn't around. She would make me stay up to watch 'Tales of the Unexpected' and 'Hammer House of Horror' films. The sound of the former still creeps me out today. I could not watch a scary movie if you paid me now.

Peter also began to make me feel very uncomfortable when he was home. He would walk into the bathroom while I was bathing, when over the age of eleven. He also walked around in a towel when he had bathed. Encouraging me to sit on his knee for a cuddle, I could feel he was happy! It made me feel sick to my stomach, and it knotted up each time, just as it used to. This is something that even now, my tummy does.

When I was around thirteen years old, Mum had enough of being a part-time wife and demanded he move back to the UK. He was reluctant but came back home and took a clerical job at a local coach builders. Mum had had suspicions that he had been sleeping with a lady in Saudi called Nola for some time, even before we went to live there. I think this had been one of her primary reasons for us going. Nola was very falsely nice to us all when we arrived. Even as a young girl, I could read her body language, and she was not comfortable around us. Mum also suspected that he had an affair with a homosexual couple who lived on the same compound. I have no idea what she based this on, although she did have a little increasing paranoia over the years. However, the breaking point came when the phone calls started coming from a young girl in London, who I remember worked at Lipton's supermarket as a checkout girl, saying she was having a relationship with Peter. I remember all the shouting, crying and name-calling on the phone going backwards and forwards between Mum and this girl. I was encouraged to talk to her, too and tell her she was destroying a family. This happened several times. I don't think the girl knew he had a wife or a family to start with, no idea how she got our number. Although the telephone pages were pretty good in those days before ex-directory.

As it turned out, he had a penchant for young girls, my cousin Georgina to be precise. She was brought up with me like a sister. Mum took her under her wing as her own mum, My aunt Linda didn't want her, and her biological dad died before she was born. Mum had lost the one true love she had because she was looking after Georgie, Paddy he was called. She was engaged to him, and he was seemingly a really devoted guy. However, his own mum convinced him over time that Georgina was Mum's secret child and that as soon as they were married, she would reveal it, and he would be stuck with her. Eventually, Paddy's mum's words stuck, and after defending herself too many times, Mum ended the engagement. Georgina was four years older than me, but still only about sixteen when it started (I suspect it could have been younger but have no proof, they had often sat cuddling on the sofa. Obviously we thought he was like a dad figure to her.) I think she had been looking for a dad, and he, at thirty-four, had been looking to take advantage of that. It still makes me shiver to think how that could possibly have initially started. Who made that move? Who thought that would be OK? Did it start as something else, something more sinister? Thank goodness it was not me, that's all I can say. Mum, had been lying in hospital, just having had a full hysterectomy, when my little brother Rick, who was about six to seven years old, walked in and asked her why Georgina was sleeping in her bed. That was that, and she discharged herself, massive scar, still in stitches and all, and then discharged Peter!

Peter and Georgina eventually moved in together, to a cosy little flat on the south side of Scarborough. My nan, grandad and aunts all still spoke to him and let him into their homes. Even though they were all disgusted by their behaviour, they were still treated as family. Mum felt betrayed by them all. Their excuse was they couldn't abandon Georgina, but in essence, they chose her over Mum. Mum never forgave any of them for that. Georgina, knowing Peter's history of infidelity, grew insecure. This manifested itself in an eating disorder. Going from a healthy size fourteen to something resembling a Chupa Chup lollypop with big '80s plastic glasses on. They even had a child together after a few years and moved to Peter's home country of Canada, where Georgina struggles to this day. Peter controls everything. She would love to leave, but he has told her everything they have is his. If she leaves, she leaves with nothing, so she buries her true feelings deep down and just gets on with it. There is a saying, "If you make your bed you should lie on it". I do believe in karma, and I guess this was hers, leading a subservient life in a country in which she doesn't feel at home. Megan, her daughter, is happy, though, and I'm sure that keeps her going.

So now it was back to Mum, my brothers and myself. Things were very tough once Peter had gone. Money was impossibly tight. We lived on food donated mainly by my uncle (who worked at McCain's), my nan, or bought at a knockdown price. The mortgage wasn't getting paid. I think social security donated a nominal amount, but Peter wouldn't give anything. Mum tried for around one-and-a-half years to keep the house, until we were eventually evicted.

Peter's maintenance was pitiful at two pounds a week. My own dad paid fifty pence a week for each child, even though Mum took him back to court when he became wealthy. He pleaded poverty too, and the court believed him. He was very proud that he always paid maintenance for his kids, and I have heard him brag about that. Nobody knew that it wouldn't have kept us in bread and milk for a day, let alone clothed us.

We got hand-me-down clothes from my cousin, although Mel was three sizes bigger than I was. I did what I could with the clothes, which were size sixteen. A long pleated skirt I shortened to a gym skirt, something I'd never had before. As I sewed the pleats, it got wider and wider, but it was mine, and nobody knew I made it. It made me feel like I fitted in. I was so proud of that skirt. I also got an old pair of my cousin Patrick's flared jeans. I never had jeans before. My friends all had them. Clearly though, flares were not going to give me any kudos in a world of drainpipe or boyfriend cut. So I sewed right up the inside of the leg, cutting away all the excess material. It was so hard with just a basic needle and some yellow cotton (the only colour we had). I sewed until my fingers were blistered, but I was so happy! I rode my bike with some of the other kids from school who were all wearing jeans. I felt great! I felt the same as everyone else. Every night I would go home and colour in the stitching that would show through as they stretched. A navy blue felt tip saw to that. I learned to be resourceful in those times. It is something that I still love today, repurposing old things and finding new homes or new ways to use them.

It was then that my OCD started, by being thrust into a situation where my mum was having a breakdown. My little brother was so young he did not know what was really going on. My middle brother was completely destroyed. To him, Peter was his dad. He had been only six-month-old when our biological dad left, and Peter was all he knew. He screamed, shouted, cried and begged my mum to take him back, but she would not. My nan, in her infinite wisdom, responded with her razor-sharp, wicked tongue, "Well he wasn't your f****** father anyway". She had such a way with words. They were straight and brutal. I think her words cut his world into pieces. After my dad's shenanigans, Mum wasn't going to take any more crap from another man. She resolved not to take Peter back.

I began not to stand on the cracks in the pavement. I couldn't stand on cigarette butts either. I thought the dirty, disgusting things would contaminate my shoes, and then my world. I hopped skipped and jumped along I couldn't walk in a straight line. I would stand in the doorways at home and make myself step over the carpet runner several times (Mum saw and used to say "Are you doing a fan dance again?" If only she knew.) I touched door handles, stair rails — many different things, many times. I kissed a little picture I had of my mum every day for so many years, as it kept her safe, I thought. My world, spiralling out of control, somehow seemed easier to handle with my little rituals. Three and four were my numbers, or multiples of three, so six and nine were OK too. I also had to do symmetry. If I touched something with one hand then I had to touch with the other. I also liked pairs and even numbers in some things. These rituals were a large part of my every day and I would feel anxiety and panic if I couldn't do them or get them right. These experiences helped me recognise OCD in my son, bless him. I followed my rituals all day, every day. Then once, in my mid-twenties, I decided to test what would happen if I didn't kiss the photo or touch the handle on both sides. What if I purposefully did the opposite of what my mind was telling me to do? I'd had enough of its control. It took a heck of a lot of willpower to overcome that urge. Alas nothing untoward happened, which was a great leap forward. I slowly took back control. The tins in the cupboard no longer all had to face forward; the knives, forks and spoons were no longer all neatly stacked the same direction. To this day, if I get stressed, it immediately heightens again. I find myself touching things with both hands, trying to do symmetry or organising something. Then I have to remind myself not to do it. I don't think it will ever fully leave.

Peter's departure had had a detrimental effect on us all, but mostly on my middle brother, Lindsay, who cried constantly and begged my mum to take Peter back. He pooped on the carpet behind the sofa and seemed to lose control. I still have an issue calling Lindsay by his birth name. He changed it to Lee James at age eighteen, a way of escaping the bullying and the bad reputation he got as Lindsay. His name change did not, however, change his behaviour. Later in life, at thirty-three years old, he alleges that he had been abused around that time and that he was told to beg Mum to take him back or it would continue. He also implicated an uncle in some abuse. However, he said this at a time when he was trying hard to stay clean but failing. He had started to take drugs somewhere around the age of sixteen, and had got into petty crime as a way of paying for them. At times, he would be so destitute that he lived on the streets, overdosing on heroin more than once. These allegations came at a time when nearly everything that passed his lips was a lie. What a shame it would have been if they were true, the boy who cried wolf on so many occasions.

The said uncle turned out to be gay, despite the fact he was married to my aunt. He had been seen cottaging at the toilets by the cemetery, not far from my other aunt's house. After that, the shame was too much, and my aunt Linda decided to starve herself to death. Soon after, he moved his boyfriend into their little bungalow. My mum had suspected he was gay for a long time. She had helped my aunt, who was chronically ill, by regularly going over to clean up, and had found a gay porn mag under his bed. He slept in a separate room to my aunt. I remember her telling me. I can't have been more than twelve, and I didn't really understand what it meant. It certainly didn't mean that my uncle or my stepdad were abusers. My brother could bullshit for England in an attempt to get what he wanted, leading to me having a severe dislike for bullshitters and lies in general. I see no place for them. If you are sparing someone's feelings because, "Yes, dear, your bottom does look big in that skirt," fair enough. Out-and-out lies, changing of stories, saying things to hurt someone on purpose? There is, and never will be, need or room for that.

I was fourteen-and-a-half, just before we were evicted, and around this time I had my first encounter with a boy I liked. His name was A*. He was quite popular in the middle school set and had a bit of a way with him, a cheeky face and loads of spikey blonde flat top hair. I developed a crush on him and somehow (I can't remember now), he found out. He asked me out and told me to meet him at the 'players' (playing fields) at the weekend. Wow, a good looking guy had showed interest in me! I was elated, to say the least, after years of my mum treating me like a boy, with terrible clothes and very short hair and her warning me, "Never grow your hair because you won't suit it." (That was her way of keeping the boys away, I'm sure). I put on my best stonewashed short denim skirt and baby-pink jumper and off I went, not knowing what to expect. As I walked up the lane, I could see a figure in the distance. Was it him? It sure was. Double wow — he actually turned up! I felt shy, but we talked and played on the swings and then sat on a bench. He made me feel very comfortable, making me laugh. And then he moved closer, leaning over towards me. My heart was so fast it was nearly beating out of my chest. I am sure he could have heard it. He put his arm around me, and pulled me even closer, and then he kissed me. I was being kissed by a boy I liked! I felt amazing. I felt like I was floating on air. Would I have something to tell Lou later!

Suddenly the heavens opened, and the rain poured down. He suggested we went to the cricket shed to shelter, which I thought was a good idea. I have never looked good in the rain, with the kind of hair that is straight at the top and curly at the bottom, when wet it goes frizzy like Wurzel Gummidge's hair. We continued to kiss, and I thought nothing of it. It was all very nice, although slightly awkward. That was until he gently manoeuvred me backwards into the corner. I hardly noticed, as I was heady from all the kissing. His hand slowly moved up my jumper cupping his hand around my bra and breast. I stopped kissing and moved his hand away. Then he slid his foot against mine and wedged my legs apart with his feet.

I didn't expect that and started to feel uncomfortable. I had a sense of foreboding, but pushed the feeling down with the thought, this is just a boy from school who I like, and he likes me. This is what boyfriends do, right? I had never had one before, so was in unknown territory, only knowing what I did from girl and boy gossip at school, which was next to nothing. Before I knew what was happening, he had unzipped his jeans, took hold of my hand and was trying to put it around his willy. I literally jumped with shock! I had never seen a boy's willy before (except my baby brother's when I used to help change his nappy and put the powder on when I was six), never mind touching one. I felt sick. I said no and pulled my hand away. It felt weird. It was soft and firm all at the same time. It made my stomach churn (that knot feeling inside was tightening once again). I tried to move, and I knew now that I had to get away. He had me wedged in the corner, feet against mine, so my skirt was tight and high around my thighs. He moved his hand under my skirt, trying to pull at my little pink panties. His mouth and tongue now very forcefully on mine, no longer kissing, just feeling disgusting.

I broke my mouth free and said NO! He did not stop for a breath. I said NO again this time with more panic in my voice, tears welling in my eyes.

He pulled my knickers to one side. He fiddled, fumbled, and tried to find the way inside me. I was filled with fear, and every bone in my body returned to the moments when I was six. I froze rigid, still saying no and pleading, with tears rolling down my cheeks. He was deaf to my cries as he tried to force himself into my dry vagina. I screamed in pain, and he recoiled back. My hymen had broken with the force of his attempt. This caused some bleeding, which shocked him enough to step back with one foot.

Without a second's hesitation, I ran. I was never a good runner, but I could have beaten Flo Jo home that day, racing down the lane, into my house and up the stairs. I bombed past my mum, made an excuse and hid myself in the bathroom, sitting behind the door to keep it shut. The tears were rolling down my face once again. What had just happened? Was that the way it was supposed to happen? Did all boys do that? Was it expected of me? Did all the girls do that? Was I frigid for saying no? What was it? A boy messing around? An attempted rape? I was backed into a corner with my feet pinned apart. Why did he not take notice of my cries and my saying 'No!'?

I had no clue what had happened to me, and I was so confused I could not speak. I could not even explain what had happened, as I didn't know. My head was spinning. I just put in a tampon to stem the blood flow, as I thought it had been my period, not knowing that tearing the hymen could draw blood, or even if that was indeed what it was. Sex education was not something I had taken much notice of, and this certainly was not part of it. Neither were we taught that it should be consensual, (which it should obviously be) or that you have a right to say no! Seeing drawings of a man's and a lady's bits, I knew what a penis and a vagina were supposed to do, but nothing prepared me for this.

I returned to school on the Monday to a few funny stares, not knowing why. A couple of weeks later, I was approached by another boy, M*, asking if I would like to go over to his house to play snooker on his new table. Little did I know that it wasn't only his snooker balls he wanted me to play with. Unknown to me, A* had gone back to school and told a lot of other boys that he had done the full thing with me, and that I was easy, so M* decided he would like to have a go.

I went to his house, having taken some snacks and drinks for our game of snooker (I was quite good, as I played a lot in the family room at the Star pub as a kid). I put them down and was quickly jumped upon and kissed. I was quite stunned, but even further stunned when I was pushed backwards onto the snooker table, as he tried to get my knickers off with one hand while his other hand was fiddling with his willy.

Luckily, I scrambled off the table while he was looking and fiddling with himself. I did another Flo Jo all the way home, in total shock that another boy had tried the same thing. It was a week or so later when I asked M* why he had done that, and he told me A* had told him that I 'put out.'

Having gone from being a tiny mouse, who still had a Sindy (English Barbie) house on the landing and who was almost invisible, I now had a reputation for being 'easy.' It was quite funny in its own way, 'cos I ceased being invisible to the girls after that. Somehow this traumatic event gave me some street cred amongst those girls who had boyfriends. There were quite a few with older boyfriends at my school.

Sometime after this, I was sick of following Nick around like a lost puppy and was feeling a little more assertive, so I decided to tell him I liked him. Something in me had changed, and I was no longer as shy. I was doing drama and had gained some confidence. I had liked him since we started to learn the trumpet together aged eleven-ish. I also sat behind him in band. I made little cushions with his name on for my bed (Adele and I used to do that for all our crushes. Hers had boys' and girls' names on, as she was never one way or another, but mine just always had 'Nick').

At GCSE options, I took history so I could be in the same class as him. I hated history at that time, especially as it turned out that World War One was to be yawningly boring for a fourteen-year-old girl. But I got to sit next to Nick, and once I had told him I liked him, I could write "I love Nick," on his books. I think it amused him and inflated his already quite large ego. For a time he would tempt me by asking, "Tell me how many guns an F16 has and I will go out with you," so I did and he still wouldn't. You see, I liked him, and he liked a friend of mine called Tracey, but she wasn't interested in him, although he was a great ego boost for her.

After a year or so, once I had found my first boyfriend, Andrew, Nick and I became very good friends. We all hung out together at school. The boys Jem, Paul, and a few others created mayhem to make the rest laugh. Ironically, in sixth form, Nick later told me he had now developed his own love for me (I think it was all down to this tiny little skin-tight black dress I had made myself).

Andrew was in the same group of guys as Nick. They were the cool guys. Kate and I used to be the only girls allowed in their group. Kate was super-intelligent and had a crush on the rebellious boy of the group, Dean. I was best friends with Kate, so I got to hang with them too.

I began to notice a geeky 'New Romantic/Mosher,' with spikey ash-blond hair and an almost blue see-through complexion. There was something strangely alluring to him. He was quirky, smart and bit awkward in his own skin, just like me. As I got to know him, I realised I liked him and told Kate, who then told Andrew. One thing led to another, and we began to meet and walk the streets in the evenings, having nowhere else to go. My first real, very own boyfriend. He lived at Osgodby, which was just up the road, but it was a scary road, unlit, uninhabited, and getting close to winter. Andrew decided he could no longer see me. Gone were the kisses at the end of my drive that lasted for hours. I think that may have been my first tears over a boy I loved. You fall in love very easily as a teen. My mum always called it puppy love.

Chapter Four

With Peter gone and Mum struggling so much, we were evicted, and the house was taken back by the bank and sold. Our beautiful, brand-new three bedroomed centrally heated semi - Mum's pride and joy - decked out in the '70s height of fashion of matching coffee and cream colours, was no longer ours. We were put on the emergency housing list and forced to take the first offered: 53 Hertford Close.

The first time Mum, Nan and I went to look at it, a piece of my mum died. It was covered in rubbish inside and out, with skull and crossbones and DIO scrawled on the walls in oil paints. It was like the unheated version of hell. My mum broke down. She felt like she had come to the end. It was down to me to see if I could help, and this was probably when I first realised I was good at being calm in a crisis and fixing things. I went to see Mrs Don, my English and Drama teacher, who also was a councillor in her spare time. I explained the situation and pleaded with her to help. She told me she didn't think there was anything she could do, but she would try. She wrangled with officials at the council and got all the rubbish removed, so we could at least move in.

There was no central heating, a gas fire in the living room and a portable Calor gas fire upstairs. Coming from the warm, comfortable home we had to leave was a shock to the system. Sharing that gas portable heater was a nightmare. I think it rarely went into my brothers' shared room, apart from bath night where I think they got a turn. I was always freezing cold. The shock hit us all. I think my mum gave up that day. She refused to bake ever again, which she had loved to do. Christmas to that point had been filled with Christmas cake, mince pies, sausage rolls, scones of all varieties and raspberry pies – all manner of freshly baked wonderments. Buffets had been filled to overflowing with vol-au-vents, half an orange foiled space stations with baby onions, pineapple and cheese, and tinned cocktail sausages with sticks coming out of them in every direction, half-bun sandwiches topped with egg mayo or tinned salty ham and plates of Party Ring biscuits. She would even plate Iced Gems, all of them upright and neatly placed next to each other (although I can't say if that was me that had organised them. If it were, they would have been in colour groups too. I was always one to sort my Christmas box of sweets into groups, counting them and carefully placing them in sections).

She was the darling of the street every New Year's Eve, my mum. Everyone in the street came to our house for eating, drinking and being merry. I was always allowed a Snowball drink of advocaat and lemonade, and often had a second or would find somebody's glass when they were not looking and have a sip or two. Nobody noticed as they were all having a great time. I was often quite merry, dancing and being silly with the other kids. We took bits of clothes and shoes off the boy who lived next door and hid them. His mum was fab, so posh and very Thatcheresque.

Those times had been innocent and sweet, and I often wondered if Mum remembered them with fondness or with bitterness, because as soon as Peter had gone, all curtains, blinds and doors were closed to her. In her hours of need, not one person came calling. She was single, and therefore posed a threat to their little suburban lives. This is quite common, as I later found out myself when I had lived in a Stepford-type community and split with my husband, Matt. Everyone shut me out, including those I called my best friends, who I had made fancy dress costumes and presents for, made my famous food for and let them pass it off as their own, and took them to the hospital when sick.

The moment I split from Matt, I never heard from them again. Well, except the very rotund husband of my friend Sue next door who thought I was now an easy target and pursued me with his pervy chat-up lines. ("Oh, you look so hot, my lovely. I'm going on a lad's trip to Edinburgh. I wish I was taking you on a weekend there instead." Yuck.)

I understood how Mum must have felt back then. I let my lost friendships pass with the wind. They weren't worth fretting over. Some people come into your life for a short time. Some are just to teach you lessons, and some are for the long distance. I think Mum remained a little sour for a long time.

She gave up the home-cooked food and turned to her new deep-fat fryer, not to use for herself but to cook for my brothers. You could grab something from the freezer and bang it in the hot deep fat, and fifteen minutes later, you had hot deep-fried sausage and skinny fries. If that wasn't the menu of the day and she had a few spare quid, it was chips, rice, mushrooms, beansprouts and curry sauce from the Chinese. The spark had left Mum back then, and it didn't return until her last few months of life. When she once again starting baking raspberry pies (my favourite thing of hers). It was as if she knew she didn't have long left and had to make them one last time.

Lindsay was lucky as he was built like a greyhound. Rick had the big Canadian genes. I, on the other hand, had been taught enough by school and the healthy bar in the canteen that I turned to toast and sandwiches and dropped all my puppy fat.

They were scary days, those first days in that house. I was never popular at school and felt like a leper for a while. Luckily, I was taken under the wings of Clarke and Kitty, two very popular boys at school who lived on the estate. They would walk home with me, and Clarke would stand and talk for a while. He was tall and sweet and made me feel safe. There was just something that was so caring about him. He made sure I got home safe every day. We had never spoken much until then.

Twenty-five years later, he would have an impact on me again, as we met through Facebook. He became my best friend, helping me through my toughest times when I left Matt, having had a similar situation himself. With his solid, truthful, slightly harsh sometimes advice, he was exactly what I needed, and he is still my 'bessie' today. If I need a verbal punch in the face, Clarke will be the one to give it to me.

It was around this time that Andrew came back into my life. Once we had moved to Eastfield, I was much closer to his house. After declaring we still liked each other a lot, we started a relationship again. Life became all about Andrew. He was my everything for a whole year. I lived and breathed Andrew. We were inseparable, except on Sundays, when there was 'Dungeons and Dragons' at Chris's house. I would ride on the back of my friend Stephen's scrambler while he whizzed up and down the field behind Chris's house trying to get Andrew's attention. Which obviously I didn't, as Dungeons and Dragons was like a military operation.

We went everywhere together Andy and I, and even had Tracey and James as 'couple' friends to go to the cinema with. Nights were spent cuddling in my room, talking and listening to music. It wasn't a mad passionate thing at all, but we were the best of friends. We spent just about every second with each other. At that time, Andrew was my grounding, my stability. He made sense when nothing else did. I needed him, and he needed me.

At about that time, I blossomed from a girl into a young woman. It sounds corny, I know, and I don't mean it in the sexual way that it sounds, but I grew my hair after having to have it short. Up to then, Mum had insisted it would not suit me, which I guess was a great ploy to keep boys away from me. I lost puppy fat too, and my curves all grew in the right places. A couple of new outfits with my school grant and I was set. By the time that school was over and sixth form had started, I was almost unrecognisable. In fact, on the first day of college, my friend Edward who had known me since I was six, did not recognise me at first. College turned out to be the start of a lesson I struggled with for a while. The 'grass is not always greener' lesson, which I think we all go through this one at some stage.

For the first time in my life, boys were actually taking notice of me. I couldn't believe it. I would think I had ink or food on my face if I saw one looking at me. I made a couple of new friends, Pam and Mel. Mel was a Goth (dyed black hair, black makeup, black clothes, heavy glasses and a lisp). She lived in Helmsley but stayed in Scarborough during the week. She was rather experienced in life compared to me. Pam was a country girl from Sleights, with streaked blonde short hair and two bunny front teeth. They were both kind and sweet to me.

On Wednesday afternoons, in our college free period Pam and I would go to the sport centre and watch the boys play. We both liked one we called 'fit bum' we never did find out his name. I sometimes played squash with this ultra-gorgeous guy called Max. He had the most amazing body and long curly dark hair, a kind of Stallone style going on. At the time, I wore boy's cartoon boxer shorts instead of knickers. My gym skirt still being the hand-made one I had made in school meant bending over in squash caused my pants to be exposed a lot. Ha! I think we liked each other, and had he not had a girlfriend (who seemed like a real sour-faced bitch) I think we could have gone out, as we talked about running away together. He was very shy, though, and it was all just banter.

By this time, things with Andrew had started to go stale. He didn't want to go anywhere or do anything. I hadn't realised at the time, but Andrew had been facing his own problems. I found myself getting bored, and along with the attention I was getting from some upper sixth guys, we decided it was time to break up. Andrew blatantly ignored me for the rest of the time I was at college.

It wasn't long before I left, as I had felt under pressure from Mum to be out earning money and looking after her, as that's what children did apparently.

Andrew's hostility didn't last. During the Christmas of 1991, Mum and I were shopping, and we bumped into Nick and Chris. I was excited as Nick still looked very cute. They invited me over to Nick's to hang out with their band. Andrew was there too. "What the hell is she doing here?" I heard him say, and he mostly ignored me. He was still very cute too.

We all agreed to meet for drinks, and by the end of the evening, Andrew was saying, "Call me," and so was Nick! My Nick, the guy who was my absolute first crush, who I followed like a puppy through school and who tormented me saying he would go out with me, but never did. Now he liked me even more than I liked him. I was torn as to what to do. I wanted to ring them both, but I had to go on at least one date with Nick. It felt like the right thing, besides I was very curious as to what that would be like, fulfilling that teenage dream.

Nick and I went out for a date. He picked me up in his car. He looked very fit, with his hair still in a long mullet, and with the warmest brown smouldering eyes, and the cheekiest smile. I was nervous. He took me for a drive to somewhere quiet and secluded. I started to think, oh this is not what I would call a date. Then things started to go from kissing to trying to get his hands down my pants within a couple of minutes. OMG I wasted so much time liking this guy! Luckily, I was wearing a fortress of thick black tights with thick black leggings over them, thick black ruffled down socks and tie up boots. An on purpose chastity belt to keep my virtue! He drove me home after being unsuccessful in his mission. I never got in touch with Nick again. A couple of years later, he turned up 'out of the blue' at my work, Vision Express. I nearly passed out with the shock when I looked up from my desk to see the next customer. He had a young lady with him, Michelle, I found out. They were shopping, and he wanted to say Hi! On his way out of the door, he turned around and signalled, "Call me," behind Michelle's back. Seriously? That will be a no! He went on to marry the girl. Luckily, they got their happy ending.

Andrew and I did hook back up in the end. I spent every weekend in Scarborough with him, travelling down after work from Vision express at the Metrocentre. We never were indoors at mine or at his. It wasn't an intimate relationship, but we were best friends again. We hung out in the cold, got tipsy in bars and ate a lot of Pizza Hut pizza.

On one occasion, our friend Jeremy was serving us in Laughton Bar, and I thought I would be clever and drink several double taboos and lemonade in quick succession. Andrew matched me. We went off for some fresh air down the gardens. Wow, it hit me all at once, and I had to stop to be sick at every bench on the way down, while Andrew held my hair, bless him. We still ended up kissing though, and spent the next six months just kissing and holding hands. Then once again, it stopped moving forward. It was no longer fun, just very cold.

At times after that, in our early twenties, we tried to find each other again. I had seen him on the street in Scarborough. I quickly tried to follow, but he disappeared. I didn't know that he had heard I was back in town and was trying to find me too. I had even gone to his workplace and stood outside for ages trying to pluck up courage to go inside. I just couldn't do it. In my head I heard him saying "What the hell are you doing here? Go away."

The next few months were spent going out at the weekend and getting very drunk.

I had started hanging around with a group of older boys and one in particular I was seeing called Heath, Hunky Heath from school! My cousin Georgina's first love crush. He was working as a bouncer and a lifeguard while doing a degree. When I spotted him, I said to Mum, "That's Heath! He is still gorgeous." She trotted towards him without further ado and said, "Julia wants to know if you are going clubbing."

"I am now" he replied and that was that!

For three months, every weekend, I was at his place, with all his mates. We drank Scarborough dry. They were fun times, although I didn't eat much but drank like a fish. We drove his speedboat out into the middle of the bay with a crate of beer, and it was a case of 'drop Julia off on the pier to get some more,' when the supply ran out. He let me drive his boat around the Marine Drive, all of us jumping up and down as I crashed the boat into countless waves at speed. I loved it. We were reckless and carefree at times, but that was who I was happy to be just for those few months.

On other weekends, we would drink from Saturday evening until the wee hours and then get up for the pubs opening on Sunday. We'd drink until they closed at lunchtime, then go down to the Regal Lady pleasure boat where Heath knew the Captain.

One of the times we sailed out and drank again, eating the remnants of a leftover buffet from the night before, the quiche would come back to haunt me. We returned to shore for pub opening time until pub closing time and a carryout of beer for the house. I was piggybacked as I could hardly stand.

I locked myself in the bathroom where the quiche had grown to enormous proportions, and let rip into the toilet. The boys broke the door down as I was making so much noise, and watched, helped or just laughed. I was supposed to be in work in several hours at the Metrocentre, a two-hour drive away, and they had promised to take me. By morning there were just bodies on the floor, none of whom I wanted to get into a car with. I was going to get into trouble.

No sooner had my wild time started than summer was over and life went back to normal. Mum had loved that time. She got to know all the boys, and they loved her too. Whenever she was out during the week in town, she was being called 'Mummsy,' everywhere she went. 'Hi Mummsy, Hey Mummsy.' One lady she knew stopped her and asked how many kids she had.

OK, enough drifting off, I am getting ahead of myself. Back to being sixteen, in the rotten house. Mum had received the proceeds of the sale of the house. It wasn't a lot of money but was enough for the social security to stop all her benefits and make her live off the capital until it ran out, so we did. Mum was never good with money, so it didn't last long. She lived day-to-day. We used a lot of taxis, had Chinese takeaways and made shopping trips to Hull, where she would buy matching dropped waist skirts and tops in every colour. She also treated herself to some cubic zirconia rings that, to a regular Joe, looked like the real thing. She started to get a little mojo back too and took me out to the pub in town a few times, I wasn't allowed to drink, but I could join in the banter and dance. When I was dressed up, I looked eighteen anyway. I remember my eighteenth birthday night out. The DJ laughed and said, "But you have been coming in here for two years!"

I think it was around this time that my middle brother started asking about our biological dad. He had heard a lot of things from my aunt Linda, who lived opposite our biological paternal grandparents. She was quite friendly with them and sat watching all the comings and goings from her bed in the living room. Mum was always getting phone calls saying things like, "Ian has been up today; he has a flash new car; he is doing this and that." It was one of these times that my brother asked if we could meet him. Mum wasn't keen, and neither was I. All my life I had been told they were all scoundrels, bad people. If I was ever naughty, which I very rarely was, I would be told I was just like the Davis's. Davis was like a swear word in our house. She had a bit of an edge, and she could be quite cold and cutting. Mum said we could only meet him if it was what we both wanted. My brother was so insistent that eventually, I gave in and said OK. I guess by this time I was a little curious. Mum got our paternal grandad Jim's phone number off my aunt Linda and rang him to pass a message along to Ian, my dad. Within hours, Ian had rung and had a conversation with Mum about seeing us. We arranged that he would pick us up at the weekend and take us all, including Mum and Ricky, for dinner.

The weekend arrived, and so did he, rolling up in his brand new BMW 7 series. Here was this man, shorter than I imagined, with brown but lightly greying hair cut into a similar style to Barry Gibb and smelling of cigarettes and expensive cologne. His eyes were brown but piercing, almost scary to me. I've always believed the eyes are the window to the soul. I can look into someone's eyes and see things that they as people don't tell you. I have never been able to do that with him. His windows were closed. He was very charming and charismatic, and I could see how he had charmed my mum as a younger lady. I could also see in her eyes that the attraction was still very much there for her. He drove us over the moors, Julio Iglesias on the CD player (I can't listen to Julio now without feeling extremely sad). He took us to Trenchers, a fish and chip restaurant in Whitby. We all ate, and then he paid and took us home. I think we were asked if we would like to see him again and we both said yes. I was very curious as to who this man was. After all the stories I had been told, I wanted to know for myself.

Ian went home and told his wife, Gill. He had been married to her for many years by now, but she had known nothing about us. Obviously it came as a great shock to her, but she agreed to meet us. A few weeks later, he picked us up and took us to the Grapes, a pub restaurant known for being good. He was quite particular about his food even then. Gill was not what I expected. She looked like someone had smacked her arse. You know, one of those naturally sour faces. I'd expected someone delicate and refined, and she certainly wasn't that, but instead was full of airs and graces. I think there is a term about being 'all fur coat and no knickers'. I could see she was not interested in my brother or Me. Gill could give daggers that would kill in an instant. She had a good lifestyle and her daughter (not biologically my dad's) to protect, so I can understand her reluctance. However, she put on a brave face and got through the meal. We returned home with a £50 note each, not knowing he would decide never to see us again.

Gill had given him the ultimatum, them or us, but not before she rang us many times in the middle of the night, calling my mum a slag and many other names (later finding out Ian had told everyone Mum had cheated on him, to save his own face) Mum let me listen to the phone call. Gill was a vindictive old witch. She manipulated it so that we had no choice in seeing him or him seeing us.

I remember many years later, Ian saying that one of the reasons he couldn't see us any more back then was because of my mum's middle of the night abusive calls. I soon put him right as to who was calling whom. He seemed embarrassed, apologised and said he had not known. Gill made sure she got what she wanted. That was us out of the picture.

Mum also met up with some old associates from when I was little. These were a baby sitter named Lizzie and her family. She started going out for nights out with them too. It was at this time that she met Barry. My poor Mum had the worst taste in men. I don't know how she did it. She was easily sucked in by smooth talk, I think. Barry was 6ft 3, built like a cocktail stick, with a moustache of which even Freddy Mercury would have been jealous. He was younger than Mum by about twelve years, nearer my age than hers. As she was around forty, this made him around twenty-eight. It later turned out that it wasn't so much her pretty face he liked, but the 'diamond' rings on her fingers. Poor Mum.

He seemed very sweet to start but was soon staying over and virtually living with us and off of us. Then the comments and looks would come any time I was dressed up to go out. He could make me feel naked even if I had had twenty sets of clothes on. He stripped me bare with his eyes. I went out and bought a lock for my bedroom door. I was never alone with him in the house as he made my skin crawl off my bones.

Barry didn't have a job, so relied on dole and handouts from Mum. He was trying to bulk up so was always ordering all kinds of supplements and powders. Mum also started to get quite sick at this time too, getting a very bad tummy all the time, as well as frozen muscles and joints. Coincidentally, the sickness left around the same time Barry did, less than two years later. I swear he was trying to see her off for her 'money'.

Maintaining all the work at college was getting harder too. Andrew and I had split up, and I was getting attention from other guys who wanted to date me for the first time. I started talking to an upper sixth form guy called Russ. He wanted very much to go out with me, but I wasn't sure. He was rather camp, and I thought he 'batted for the other side'. He invited me to a party at a friend's house. They all lived at the posh end of town, and it was all a bit intimidating for me. I have always struggled with feeling good enough for anyone, even to this day. I think that ultimately it is due to the constant rejection from my own father. If your own dad can't love you or want to be in your life, then there must be something wrong with you. I really have struggled with this. I know that it is something wrong with him, not me, but sometimes I have felt lower than low, unlovable, a nobody, a mistake, I was an unplanned and unwanted child. Uncomfortable in my own skin sometimes. I am getting better with it, though.

It was at this party I met Adam. I knew of his brother from the upper sixth. He always looked down his posh nose at me. I went to the party and met Adam on the stairs, and we had an instant attraction. He was a student at Leeds Poly. Nobody in my family had ever gone to Poly or Uni. I had little idea what it was all about. I broke it to Russ that I wasn't interested in him but Adam. That made him cry. Oh God, that was awkward. Sitting on a bench not knowing what to do. I'd just made a boy cry. I told the truth, but it felt horrible. I started seeing Adam and was soon invited to his house for tea. Both his teacher parents grilled me on my plans, and why I had chosen to re-sit English literature at GCSE, having passed English language. Little did they know I had no real idea either and had no guidance from anyone. I had bumbled through my education, making decisions based on boys or other random things.

English literature was far better the second time around though. I enjoyed it, along with German and Sociology at A level and mid-level French.

I was quite good at German and French, even though I skipped a lot of my French lessons at GCSE. I still don't know the alphabet but managed to get a B! Sociology? I have no idea why. I think I overheard a friend talking about it. It was full of complicated words and I didn't understand any of it. Most of the time, I gazed out of the window. I hadn't a clue where I was going educationally. The only thing I wanted to do was act, but that was not a possibility. Mum had flat out refused to allow me to go away to a drama college, even though I was a natural. She did to me what her mum had done to her. She had been offered a job in Germany dancing when she was a young woman, and my nan refused to let her go. Mum had always wondered what would have happened in her life had she been allowed to do so. I don't think she saw it as the same thing, but it was. I was more use at home, earning money to bring into the family kitty. I took a part-time job in a shoe shop to supplement my college and home life.

Had I the choice, I would have sunk under the table that day at Adam's house. I felt so tiny and small that I'm sure they wouldn't have noticed. I can remember nothing else but that grilling at the table. I went off on the bus to see him at Poly once term started again. He met me off the bus, and I stayed at the halls of residence with him, getting a z bed from one of the other students and being fed some pasta one of the other girls made. That night, when I slept in Adam's bed, I knew what was expected but hadn't a clue what my part was supposed to be. I lay there and let it happen. I was numb to it, with no feelings. It wasn't horrible, but it suddenly felt very wrong. It was just all too much, and Leeds seemed a long way away. I didn't see him again.

Within weeks, I had met Derek, a Geordie lad from Newcastle on a night out in Scarborough with a few friends. He told me he was twenty-one. I told him I was eighteen. In reality, he was nineteen and I was seventeen. He was visually gorgeous, tall and slim with big broad shoulders, blond floppy fringed hair like Jason Donovan, and big blue eyes. He was also kind, sweet and loving. We saw each other across the dance floor, and that was that.

The first night I met him, I took him home. He had nowhere to stay as their hotel room, and car had been taken over by bonking friends. I have had a tendency all my life to take in waifs and strays. I knocked on Mum's bedroom door at 2 am and asked her if this complete stranger could stay. In her half-asleep/half 'spaced out from temazepam' mind, she said yes, as long as he was downstairs. I made him a bed on the floor in the living room, put the fire on, got him a spare quilt and cuddled up to him all night. From that point onwards, we were inseparable.

He was a private investigator back home in Newcastle. To me, a little country girl from the backwater of Scarborough, that seemed very exotic and almost romantic. He had a 'Bruce Willis from Moonlighting' thing going on, something he had practised in front of the mirror, he later told me. I still can't watch Bruce Willis without thinking of Derek. He drove down to Scarborough every weekend. My mum adored him, and he adored her. I left college as I couldn't take any more, and Mum had been pressuring me about bringing money into the house. I just worked my part-time job at Timpson's shoe shop.

Chapter Five

For a year we had so much fun, then Derek decided he no longer wanted to make the journey to Scarborough every weekend. It was break up or move to Newcastle. So I moved. Mum was gutted, but the big city and getting away from Scarborough seemed too exciting to miss for me. I just packed my stuff and went. Derek's dad arranged a little bedsit for us to share. It was small but sweet in an apartment block meant for single working people. I eventually found work at Chelsea Girl as it was changing to River Island. Those first few months were so happy. Food was either takeaway (as we were out and about private investigating) or my speciality of a plate of beans with two floating Bernard Matthews turkey burgers on top. There was only so much you could do with a £10 food budget and no cooking skills. It was hilarious when his friend came round for tea!

Things started to get a little eye-opening living with a boy for the first time. He took his clothes off in the evening and left them in a pile where they fell, then put them back on in the morning more creased than ever. He didn't brush his teeth nor squeeze his spots. The newness and excitement eventually started wearing off, and I wondered if I had actually done the right thing. We visited Scarborough as often as we could. Mum wasn't doing well without me there, and Barry was being a pain in the bum too. One weekend, Nan and Grandad's fiftieth wedding anniversary, they invited all the family up from Norfolk. Mum and her sisters had spent a lot of her youth there, and it was quite a close family. Co had also come over from Holland. He had been an exchange student when they were all at school. He had written and visited every year since they were teens. He had been in love with my aunt Ginny, the eldest of the sisters. She was never interested in Co and instead found love with my uncle Malcolm. Co seemed a nice man. He called Nan and Grandad. *Mum* and *Dad*. He was a big rotund man, with white-blonde hair in a comb-over, with milky-white skin and sky-blue eyes, but always sweating heavily. He rode from Holland every year on his Honda Goldwing. It was a marvellous thing! He always seemed to have money and brought presents for everyone. I can't remember anymore what his job was, but he was doing OK for himself. But he never did find love.

Mum looked beautiful as always and dazzled everyone with her light-hearted humour and gorgeous smile. The evening was going well. We were allowed into the front room, which was always kept for best, and the sisters had provided a buffet. Mum was close to her cousin and her husband and had been talking to them for a while. Her cousin went off to the toilet, leaving

Mum and Keith alone talking. Barry had been watching like a hawk the whole time it seems. As soon as Mum laughed at something Keith said, Barry threw his drink at her in front of everyone, accusing her of flirting with her cousin's husband and humiliated her. I hadn't seen the event but heard the commotion. That was it. Julia to the rescue. I immediately took over.

Barely eighteen years old and tiny in comparison, I took hold of him, gave him the blunt end of my tongue and kicked him out of the door. I marched him the whole mile home, shouting abuse at him all the way! Big Co was a little way behind huffing, puffing and trying to keep up, as nobody else dared to follow. I pushed him in the door, ordered him to get his stuff, then threw him out and took his key. Job done! Thank goodness for that. I learned quite young that your tongue can be as powerful as any muscle that you have. I am not tall of stature, but I can give a good tongue-lashing or lecture.

It wasn't long before loneliness somehow took hold of Mum again and she let Barry and his sorry ass back in. I never could understand that, but I guess that to her somebody was better than nobody. Within weeks, he had somehow asked her to marry him, and within a couple of months, they were married. She seemed to be on a rollercoaster even she couldn't stop, but didn't know there was a brick wall at the end of it!

I remember that day in such a surreal way, as if it never happened and was a figment of my imagination, one of those times that play out very slowly, but she did indeed become Mrs Gibson, a name she hated for the rest of her life. Within six weeks, she was heading for a divorce, and he was heading for the hills with what little money she had left (about £1000). She blamed me. I had after all abandoned her, and she was lonely, she said. I think she felt naïve and stupid. Everybody had warned her about him, but she had a stubborn streak, my mum. She didn't listen to good advice.

Quite soon, word had travelled across the water to Co in Holland, and he rang Mum offering his support. She was always fond of Co as a person, but it was definitely in a 'friend' sort of way. He was, after all, massively overweight and always looked like he was literally melting. Over the coming weeks, my middle brother had started to act up. It was yet another change for someone who struggled to cope with it. He swapped his brand new bike for an old knackered computer, in order to gain a friend, which didn't happen. He struggled to make friends, was nicknamed 'Jugs' because of his sticky-out ears and always seemed to be alone. I realise now it was very likely that he had ADHD, but it wasn't diagnosed so much in those days. Instead he was called 'hyperactive'. He couldn't concentrate on anything for very long, but I think, ultimately, it was after our dad shunned us that he just felt at a loss within himself. He needed a man in his life and thought stepdad Peter was his dad until my nan put that right. Our biological father had always told us in not so many words that we weren't good enough and that money was far more important. It made a massive impact on my brother as a person.

From that day onward, he was never right, and I think it broke him. He was very much a man's boy. He sought solace in the wrong company and started to get into petty crimes, nothing of any major scale but just hanging with the wrong crowd. Mum was worried for him, and I think she must have talked about this with Dutchman, Co, in one of their phone calls.

Before I knew it, on my next weekly call to her from Newcastle, she told me Co had asked her to move to Holland with my brothers. Here was this self-proclaimed bachelor asking Mum to give up her council house, benefit claims (hard to get back once you give them up) and all her possessions, and move to Holland with him, as a friend. Her house was certainly a step down from our previous beautiful home in Cayton, but still represented stability.

He said he would look after her and the boys and was sick of seeing the hardship she was going through. WOW! That was a bit of a shock to hear.

Mum asked me what she should do. I hadn't a clue, but I didn't trust Co's 'friend' intentions at all. Mum insisted that he said it would be separate rooms etc. and he just wanted to help her out and give her a break from the hardship she had been enduring. I told her she should go with her gut feeling. I'm not sure what the gut was saying, but within weeks she had given away most of her possessions (funny how you seem to be very popular when you give stuff away) and was on board a ferry to the Hook of Holland with a few boxes of treasured photos and mementoes. That was all she had to represent the last forty-two years of her life. She was to be met by Co's brother, Donald, who it seemed was a very nice man — unlike his brother, she would later find out.

A few weeks after she arrived in Holland, Derek and I went on a magical mystery tour by coach to Amsterdam. It took about twenty-four hours but was a brilliant journey. I think it cost us £15 each. Fantastic! Co was going to pick us up in Amsterdam. What he didn't tell us was there were two stops, and we got off at the wrong one. There was no sign of Co, so we found the train station and took a train to Kirsenbogart and a taxi to the house. Mum was delighted to see us, but in the days before mobile phones, Co was not amused when he got home to find us there. He stomped around and made us feel uncomfortable. Mum made us feel better with her newly found Gouda cheese toasties, yum scrum! It quickly came to light that she had been duped and the circumstances in which she found herself were less than desirable. When Co said 'friend', he meant girlfriend, housemaid and virtual prisoner. He only had his Goldwing, so they could only get about by public transport. Mum wasn't the most confident person out on her own in a foreign country. (In Saudi, it was law to be accompanied by your husband when you were out). I think she only left the house if Donald came to pick them up to go shopping.

My brothers were enrolled into school, and they quickly made friends, although my middle brother once again found the wrong crowd. Even speaking a different language, the wrong crowd of people find each other. It's as if it was stamped on his head. Once my little adventure was over, and Derek and I returned to Newcastle, I got a call a couple of weeks later stating they were coming home. My brother Lindsay had shot someone with an air rifle, Co had decided he no longer wanted to have responsibility for him, and Mum had decided she no longer wanted more or less to prostitute herself to a man who held her virtually captive, who literally made her stomach churn when he touched her. It was, I think, a mutual decision all round. Donald picked up Mum and the boys and returned them to the ferry with tickets paid for, but not a penny in her purse. I have no idea why or how she left without her few treasured possessions, but they were sent to her later and were mostly in bits by the time they arrived. She blamed Co and said he had smashed them, but I think they just were not parcelled or protected at all and had a rough journey. She had started to get a real persecution complex, and she thought people did things against her on purpose. What she didn't realise until the last few months of her life was by thinking that, she was actually creating it, making it happen.

Here she was on the shores of England again, homeless, without a stick of furniture or a penny to her name. Long gone were the days of bagging yourself a cushy council home, or even a shitty one, in a hurry. They all moved in with Nan and Grandad, which was not the easiest of things to do. It was a tiny home, and although bedroom space wasn't too bad, Nan wouldn't let anyone in the spacious front room, so all five of them had to live in the tiny kitchen and galley dining room which they used as a living room.

The social security had no sympathy whatsoever. Mum had given up her house, so wasn't entitled to another, and she had given up her benefits. She would have to go right through all the rigmarole right from the start, and then wait for a decision. She was put on the emergency housing list, but that consisted of B&B rooms and dodgy, damp, squalid flats that people with a choice wouldn't touch. After some weeks at Nan's – and I think out of sheer desperation – she took a one bedroomed flat on North Marine Road. It was up lots of stairs, with a tiny living room, a kitchen all-in-one and a bedroom that the boys shared. Mum slept on the sofa. It wasn't ideal, but at least she got away from the nagging and whinging that my nan and grandad gave her. Even after encouraging her to go to Holland (as Grandad could make some cash selling Mum's furniture), she got a big bunch of 'told you so' when she got back. Although they still had some of her furniture and things, she was never offered them back. This was disgusting, as Mum had given and given to Nan and Grandad when we lived at Cayton and had a bit of money. It was just a few months that she lived in that squalid place before the house next door to my aunt Ginny came up for rent. The landlord was an old friend they had known as teenagers too, so worked out well. It was unheated, plain and drably furnished but at least it was a decent area to live.

She settled into life there with the boys, and I felt a little more assured because at least she had her sister next door. My middle brother, on the other hand, started to get out of control. Since returning from Holland, he seemed hell-bent on self-destruction. After our dad's rejection of him, he decided it would be a good idea to go and try to find his family, as that would be the nearest thing. Out of all the Davis family members he could have found – and there are lots of them – it was Dad's younger brother, Steven, who was a ne'er-do-well. I'm told he has a good heart, but his lifelong drug addiction often clouded his judgement.

Lindsay was the kind of kid that liked to please because he thought it made him friends. He thought Steven was one of them. I don't know, and never will know, the circumstances surrounding these early days with Steven. All I know is that my brother started on a path that would destroy any chance of a normal life for him, and would see his cousin Matty, Steven's son, dead from an overdose. Mum noticed things like her temazepam (sleeping tablets) going missing. That was devastating to her, as she couldn't sleep without them. She couldn't really sleep with them but needed them nonetheless.

Of course, this is when the lies started. At a young age, he could swear on his, yours or anyone else's, life that he hadn't done something. He was so convincing that he even convinced himself. I guess this was a genetic trait, as my dad, in a conversation many years later, told me he had never laid a finger on anyone in his entire life and that I the little four-year-old tot of a girl was a liar. To be fair, my dad was always drunk when he hit Mum. I know this was no excuse, but I have had my own share of my drunk dad, as I will explain later.

So my brother had been providing his 'friends' with 'wobbly eggs' as they called them, and joining them in petty crimes. He once got caught stealing a bunch of girl's hair accessories. That made me laugh. He was hardly a master criminal, at least for now! How and when the harder drugs started, I'm not sure, but I know it wasn't long. He hung around at Steven's house a lot as did a few other youths, one of them being Matty, just a young teenager himself. I think in those days Lindsay was close to Matty. Sometimes strange things help form relationships with people, even drugs.

Poor Mum was always down at the police station trying to sort him out. She threatened him left right and centre. Ultimately, he knew, and so did she, that it was all pointless and that he would do what he wanted. When he turned sixteen and left school, he was turfed out for the first time. I think at first there was a bit of peace for Mum, but then she started to worry a lot, and that affected her sleep even more. He started to get a bit of a reputation around town. Mum was horrified and embarrassed. He decided to make a fresh start, change his name to Lee and move to Leeds, so for now, Mum had a little peace. I was heading to Scarborough most weekends, and Mum and I had a few nights out. It was my way of helping her relax and forget her rubbish situation. It was also a way to get away from my own situation.

I had found a new job! I had been talking to a lady shopper in River Island, and she turned out to be the manageress at Vision Express. I went for an interview and got the job straight away. I was dispensing glasses the very first day. I was a natural and I loved it.

Things were not going so well with Derek. Don't get me wrong, he was the nicest chap, and my mum loved him, but I was so young, and he had become like my best friend. We went 'private investigating' together in my spare time, and ate picnics or Chinese food in the car while following and watching people. We even had our language, but the chemistry of boyfriend and girlfriend was gone. I loved him dearly, but in that brother/ best friend way. Eventually January the first came round one year, and he asked me, "Do you love me?" It had gotten so messy, my head had had enough, and I told him "No."

He moved in with his Mum and Dad and gave me two weeks to leave. I was barely twenty, and I hadn't a clue what to do. I rang my dad to see if he could advise me, he said he would come up at the weekend. He booked us a hotel for a couple of nights. Took me out for tea, talked about himself all night, then got up and left the next morning. Leaving me with a night in a hotel room then nowhere to go. Thankfully the deputy manager at work said she was renovating her grandmother's house in Chopwell, and I could rent a room from her, which sounded like a good plan. What she forgot to tell me was that it was uninhabitable, not even with running water. I arrived all alone at night with no electricity. It was shocking. I camped on a mattress on the floor. The next morning I went to work and told my friend Karen what had happened, to which she immediately said, "You can't live there." She told me Paul and she would collect my stuff and that her mum and dad would let me stay with them. Stan and Maureen became like surrogate parents to me. Stan an imposing figure with long, grey hair and a long, grey beard, very much a dad. He tells me to this day I am still a daughter to him.

Maureen was a beautiful woman who clearly passed her looks down to her daughters. They were the kindest people I knew, compering and hosting charity events. Maureen was an amazing seamstress and made crinoline-type dresses for all their re-enactments. Stan took us to the train station every morning in his VW camper van. We had many evenings of movies and carpet picnics, and weekends looking after Karen's baby niece, Nicola. I was welcomed into the family. It was a beautiful, safe place to be. I never had a proper family before. Sundays were Paul's mum and dad, Flora and John's full family Sunday dinner. Little Gran was there, always making everyone laugh. We drank wine with dinner, which was quite posh for me. We usually went for pre-drinks to the pub, so we all fell asleep after dinner.

As I was leaving the apartment building I lived in with Derek for the last time, I saw one of the guys who lived there in the lift. He was really handsome in a rock and roll way. I didn't know his name but swooned every time I saw him. He saw me carrying my things, and I told him I was moving out. "That's a shame," he said. As the lift doors opened, and I went to leave, I said, "Well, you know where I work if you want to pop in." Although I wasn't sure he did know where I worked other than the Vision Express badge I was wearing. The next day, hair tied up and not looking my greatest, I turned around, and there was a vision of gorgeousness standing there. I nearly fell over as my knees went wobbly! WOW! All the girls were giggling and chatting amongst themselves. It wasn't often that we had such a gorgeous guy in the shop and he was approaching me! Ian turned out to be his name. He made the excuse that he had come for new glasses, although I had never seen him wear any. I convinced him that I should make a special order of some frames for him to try on, so that I knew he would return, but by the end of the conversation, we had established that we were both free Thursday and agreed to a date. He came to pick me up from Stan and Maureen's in his white Astra. I answered the door, and there he stood. Five-foot ten, and as stunning as any rock god on TV, with long dark hair, chiselled features, stunning blue eyes and a huge dazzling white smile and a body only a gym instructor would have, being well-toned but not overly muscular. All the girls loved him, and he knew it.

I was in my curly highlighted blonde phase, backcombed to the hilt. I wasn't very good at makeup and didn't know about fancy clothes. Next to him, I didn't feel worthy. What was he doing with me? Twelve years older than me, he was the only guy I have ever dated with such an age gap. He had been married, had lived in Johannesburg, and it seemed he had 'been there and done that'. He was domesticated too. He cooked, cleaned and ironed, packing me a little lunch for work the next day when I stayed over. He never wanted to go far, except one night he took me to the rock bars in town, which was unexpected as I was wearing leggings and a denim shirt. I noticed the girls were all over him, and he lapped up the attention. One girl even came over to tell me how lucky I was to have him! As cute as it all was, after a few months, I started to get bored of the routine of just staying over at his place and not going anywhere or having any deep conversation. I was so paranoid about how I looked, I went to bed in my makeup and got up when he fell asleep to wash it off. Before he woke in the morning, I was up and made up again with hair done. It was exhausting trying to be perfect all the time, but I did not think he would look twice at me without my hair and makeup done, as I had little confidence in myself. I think I was his very own blow-up doll. I was still so inexperienced I just did everything he told me to do.

A couple of months later, I ended things with Ian and moved out of Stan and Maureen's. I found a little room to rent in Gateshead in a shared flat. The two guys who lived there worked away from home, so went away every weekend. I couldn't tell you their names, and I don't think I ever said more than 'Hi' to them. I loved my attic bedroom. I had a small portable TV, a ghetto blaster I borrowed from work and an iron and ironing board, so all my clothes were neatly ironed in my wardrobe. My bed was under a skylight so that I could see the stars at night. I often caught the bus home with Dave from work, who used to say we had a love-hate relationship. We had that flirty – but sometimes not so nice – thing going on. He hated the perfume I wore, as I'd changed from body shop Vanilla (which everyone said smelled like cookies and made them hungry) to Calvin Klein Escape. What I didn't know about perfume at the time was that, like people with poor hygiene, you stop smelling it on yourself. I sprayed that stuff liberally several times a day, much to Dave's dismay, as he hated it. It smells like dry ice, he would say. I can't say I've ever sniffed dry ice, but he was offended by my smell which made me laugh all the more.

I also started to go to Preston to see my dad on the occasional weekend. My friend Ashlynne had a boyfriend, Neil, who worked at BNFL and shared a house with his mates. It was a good excuse to see my dad if he was free, which on only one occasion he was. Well technically, it was a lad's night out that I gatecrashed, deciding to drink everyone's drinks as well as my own and get very drunk. Dad then took us all for an Indian meal, something I had never had before. He recommended I start with vivid red chicken tandoori, and he ordered champagne for everyone. After my first glass, my chicken came. It tasted great, but what was that 'gurgling' feeling in my tummy? Oh blimey! I rushed up the stairs to the toilet, where everything came back up. Bleurgh! I wasn't feeling too great.

I had a terrible habit in those days of forgetting to eat, then drinking. Not a good combination. At the end of the night, I got back to my dad and his wife's home, where I was staying, and put myself to bed with a glass of water. I drifted off to sleep in that 'spinning' place we all go to at the end of a great night. Sometime in the early hours, the tandoori chicken once again decided it was not staying in. I woke with a fright as I vomited in my sleep. Hand quickly over the mouth, I ran to the bathroom. They put red food colouring in that chicken, you know.

I walked back into the guest bedroom only to find my hand had not caught all of the spray, and there was a rather large patch of very red vomit on the floor. Back to the bathroom, I grabbed what in my confused state was just something to mop the mess up, but in reality turned out to be one of Gill's very expensive and very fluffy towels. The very thick, almost shag pile, carpet had soaked up all the red, as had now the fluffy towel. I dropped back into bed, finished my sleep and rearranged the towel on the floor in the morning as I rushed out the door when Ashlynne peeped the horn. Gill was, as Ashlynne described her, a 'po-faced old witch'. I was scared of her, but I never did see her again after that. I'm sure my dad got a right old telling off!

The only other weekend I remember around that time of my few weekends to Preston with Ashlynne was a fine and sunny Friday afternoon. We would both have Friday off, so got to Preston Thursday night and back to work for Saturday morning, then back to Preston until Monday morning. Anyway, this beautiful day we decided to go for an afternoon drink by the river. We found a pub called The Ribble Pilot with big windowsills overlooking the river. We plonked ourselves on one of those, chatted away and drank. I was on Cointreau and fresh orange (my dad's influence), and she was drinking vodka and fresh orange. The idea was we would have a few and then call Neil to pick us up. The afternoon flew by, the table seemed full of empty glasses, and I'd done my usual thing of not eating. We decided it was time to go home and eat, so we called Neil. No answer. We had another and called again. No answer, so Ash, in her infinite wisdom, decided she was in a fit state to drive home. I was not in a fit state to decide otherwise. I am not advocating drinking and driving in any way. It was incredibly stupid, and we were very lucky not to have been involved in an accident.

Back at the house, the boys were now home and cooking a chicken and cream concoction in the kitchen. I remember them looking at me strangely, probably because I was very drunk. Ash grabbed a bottle of wine and a chunk of brie and went upstairs to let the boys get on with their domestic duties. I couldn't stomach the wine or the brie. For some random reason, I don't know how it started, but Ash and I started kissing. I had never kissed a girl before. Nowadays it's more normal, but it was quite something back then. We started to take our clothes off and discovered we both had the same lace body stocking on but in different colours, which we found hilarious. We fell onto the bed laughing, at which point Neil came upstairs to tell us dinner was ready and his chin nearly hit the floor. Haha! I didn't feel like eating by this point. I climbed into my bed.

That night, Cointreau started to re-visit me, and I was running around the house completely naked and not sure where my underwear had disappeared to. Ash was following me, trying to cover me in a quilt, while I was vomiting so loudly that nobody could sleep. Needless to say, when she drove off to work the next day, I was way too ill to go. Instead, the boys took me to Blackpool pleasure beach where I ate a giant bockwurst and went on the corkscrew rollercoaster. That seemed to turn my stomach back round the right way ready for another night out when Ash got back from work. I was never a crazy kid, but I did have some fun times. I think you need those to look back on as you get older, to prevent a mid-life crisis.

I decided to go down to Scarborough and see Mum for a week. I hadn't been visiting her much, due to living between Stan and Maureen and Ian's. I packed my little half-moon suitcase and vanity bag Mum had bought me and off I went on the bus into Newcastle, the express to Middlesbrough and then onto Scarborough. It was a long journey but always worth it. I had a lovely week with Mum and took her out on Saturday night as a treat. In the nightclub I noticed a young guy, very handsome, and he was staring over at me. He asked me to dance, so I did. His name was Russell, and he was a farmer.

He was everything Ian wasn't, the complete opposite to be fair. For starters, he was two years younger than I, rather naïve, and had barely left North Yorkshire. Russell thought I was this amazing girl from the city. He was full of massive enthusiasm for me. I agreed to see him again.

It lasted for six months with Russell. I had moved back to Scarborough too and had realised this was a massive mistake. While I was there, it was my twenty-first birthday. My dad said I could have a party and I held it at the function room of the Lord Nelson pub on the seafront. A large group of my Vision Express friends came down to celebrate with me, which was fantastic. Dad put money behind the bar and gave me raffle tickets to dish out for free drinks. I think I drank the bar dry of Mirage and lemonade. I just kept going around giving everyone bottles of beer.

I don't think many people paid for drinks that night. As I danced and got drunker, I kept nipping off the bathroom to make sure I looked OK. I hairsprayed my hair so much it took days to get it all out. The pictures of my twenty-first birthday hair are hilarious. My dad was happy to throw me a party on one condition, which was that he could bring his girlfriend. What? he had a girlfriend and a wife? Oh my! She seemed sweet enough. Denise was young and very naturally pretty. I only got my party because of her as he wanted an excuse to get away from Gill. She seemed humble and not after his money. She hid it well it would seem. Dad eventually left Gill and moved in with Denise. That was after running two households and families (Denise had a son) for at least two years. No wonder he never had any time for me.

Russell's age in the end became an issue. He was just so immature. The final nail in that coffin was when we agreed to share a Chinese takeaway that I paid for. My idea of sharing was two plates, two forks or one bite each in turn. His was to put it all on one plate with one fork, and with plate held up to his mouth, just keep eating. Half way through, after I started getting annoyed, he held it right under my nose and said, "Want some?" My tolerance ended there. I knew it was over. I've just never been able to stand greedy people. He left, and I wrote a 'Dear John' letter to him. I was never any good at breaking up with boys. I told him I was either moving to Israel on a moshav (which my friend had invited me to do, and I was considering) or back to Newcastle. Either way, it was over.

The decision, in the end, had been an easy one. Tel Aviv at that time was suffering from a period of unrest. I had also heard that an old school friend I didn't want too much contact with was going to Israel. So decision made, it was back to Newcastle. Ian, my boss at Vision Express, kindly gave me my job back and I found a little house share with two guys in Kingston Park. I started seeing one of the guys from work. I was young and didn't really believe the 'don't mix work and pleasure' rule. Mark was cute, with boyish good looks, thick brown spikey hair and doe-brown eyes and Bambi length long eyelashes. He worked hard on his body and totally rocked a Levi top and jeans. He was short, though. Barely an inch or two taller than me, which was new to me, having been with six-foot-two Derek. I had never heard of 'short man syndrome', but I sure understand it now. His dad, even shorter than Mark, was an angry guy, with a massive chip on his shoulder, especially when he drank, which seemed to be quite often. His mum was little and feisty with short ginger hair a squeaky voice and called everyone 'hinny'. I don't think there was an abundance of love in that household, but she did make a great Sunday dinner which we went for most weeks. Mark was quickly a permanent fixture at Kingston Park. We spent most of the time in my room, as I wasn't too keen on the two guys I lived with. Harry, the one whose house it was, was older, and it definitely felt like his house. The other, Simon, worked opposite shifts to me, so I never saw him.

I quite quickly started to fall ill. I seemed to be getting a few water infections, which, despite my kidney issues, had never happened to me before. I found out through those constant infections that I was pregnant! We hadn't been together more than a couple of months, and it was a shock. Feeling as if I had no other choice, I decided to keep the child. I later realised this had been a conscious decision by Mark to try and get me pregnant. He was a very insecure man and thought I was too good for him and that I would leave. To him, a baby would keep us together.

I grew wearier and wearier and got infection after infection. I was carried out of the house on a stretcher more times than I ever walked out. Each time the pain pointed to appendicitis, but each time it was my kidney. By this time, I was barely eating, barely working. My kidney problems were going to make it extremely difficult. I was twenty-one, my mum lived in Scarborough, and my dad didn't even know where I lived. I felt alone with one of the most difficult decisions of my life. If I carried on, I risked my own life.

I had to make the decision to save myself. As it was, my left kidney was already down to ninety-three per cent failure. It was creating infections, scarring my decent kidney, and it needed to come out ASAP. I mourn that child every twenty-fifth of August. He would be twenty-six now.

The nurse had come to me afterwards and told me the baby had been bigger than they expected. I didn't know what that meant. Was it all the antibiotics? Was it older than they told me on the scan? Why did she tell me that? She had given an identity to the life that had been inside of me - she had seen it. Still to this day, those words haunt me. I will carry guilt around with me forever. I had decided that my baby would have been called Jacob. I just knew it had been a boy. I swore to the unborn child that one day I would have a boy and in his honour I would call him Jacob. That is exactly what I did.

October came around, and my left kidney was removed. It was a straightforward operation, and the doctors were pleased. My dad visited the day before my operation, in very typical Ian style. He didn't want to risk bumping into my mum, I guess. He brought me chocolates, although he knew I would be nil by mouth. Then he proceeded to open them and hand them round the nurses. He always liked to give the impression of a kind and generous man, my dad. He didn't see that giving away my present, and having to watch other people eat them while he batted his eyelashes at the nurses, was not a nice thing for me. I was starving. Half an hour later he was gone, it was his token visit to say he cared. I hadn't even had my operation, but he wasn't going to stick around. Even major life-threatening surgery removing one of my vital organs couldn't make him do that. I didn't see him again for over a year. I woke up from the operation feeling really grumpy. Mum was there with flowers and was trying to unwrap them to put them in a vase.

The sound of the crackling paper was like high pitched thunder and lightning in my ears. It was driving me crazy in my morphine spaced out head. In a demonic raspy voice, I tried to shout, "Put the flowers down." Then zonked out again in a drugged-up haze. I remember seeing my scar for the first time when the surgeons came round to inspect their work, congratulating each other on such a neat scar. All I saw was that if I moved slightly, it looked like the fluted edge of a Cornish pasty. How was it going to heal straight? It looked so big for such a small kidney. They told me they'd struggled to find it at first as it was so small, and had to negotiate an extra set of ribs that they found I had. It seemed to amuse them.

I started to recover over the next six weeks. Just before the op I had bought my first little house. It was a stone-built, mid-terrace worker's cottage on a very steep hill. It had a little galley kitchen, all clad in pine tongue-and-groove, which made it feel like a Swedish sauna, and a very cold, tiled top-to-bottom downstairs bathroom, but I loved it. I had a home, and it was mine. I bought the most ridiculous furniture, but I was only twenty-one/twenty-two. I had no idea, so I had green, red and blue striped settees, blue floral wallpaper and borders on the walls. My biggest treat was a pine four-poster bed in my bedroom. It wasn't expensive, but I just adored it and hung net curtains down the sides and tied them back with big bows. I felt like a princess every time I went to bed. I was so happy.

I realised quite quickly though that things were going wrong with Mark. He had started to become both selfish and domineering. I was discouraged from seeing my friends, and I could never go anywhere without him. Consequently, I started to lose confidence in myself. We had been together about two years when I realised it was over. He moved out and took the stripy settees with him, but not before he had kept coming back to taunt me. His actions left me with a dislocated little finger I didn't even realise I had. If you back me in a corner, it would seem I am my father's child. I punched him in the face, which was the one and only time I have ever hurt someone like that.

I was very happy on my own. I felt strong and independent, paid all my bills, looked after myself and went about my normal everyday life. One day at work, my friend Karine suggested I get a lodger. She thought it would make things much better financially and I would have someone else at home for company. She already had a girl in mind who worked at the gift shop along the way.

Wendy was lovely. She was small, curvy and bubbly, like a little, giggly fairy. She worked in one of the Italian restaurants in town as well as part-time at the gift shop, so she spoke fluent Italian. She taught me my first Italian swear word and how to tell someone they had a small willy, which was so much fun when you were on a night out. Wendy seemed fantastic. We agreed she moved into my spare room a few days later. Things were going well, and I had applied for a job with United Arab Emirates to work on their new fleet of 777s. Having loved aircraft since I was ten years old, it seemed like the ideal career change. I already had experience of the Arab way of life from my time in Saudi as a girl. It was all very exciting.

Chapter Six

Just a few short weeks later, on a night down Newcastle Quayside with Karine, my life was to change completely. We were in Julie`s nightclub, the popular place for the young and trendy at the time. There was a long line of people walking up the stairs and a long line coming down, everyone laughing, talking and generally being drunk. Suddenly both queues came to a grinding halt. I looked up to see what was happening, and glanced across at the person opposite me in the other queue. All I saw was this huge smile and sparking blue eyes. It was worthy of the Cheshire cat in Alice in Wonderland. It was that much of a smile. Wow, this guy was handsome.

The lines started moving again, and he disappeared. I went to find Karine and tell her. Searching around, we finally came across him, and she knew him. They had been talking a few weeks before. "You are Matt," she said. He looked at her, bemused that she knew his name, as he had no idea who she was. Karine was stunning - everyone tried to talk to her. Older than me with two kids and married she was a pro at flirting, but the one-carat rock on her finger, and two girls in private schools told where her priorities lay. "This is Julia," she said, and then she left.

Matt and I talked, and he offered me a drink at the bar. I tried to be cool and order a cola, the same as he did. Then he fell down the steps, at which I burst out laughing and figured that was probably his first soft drink of the evening. Taller than me with a solidly built frame, he looked ripped in his tight t-shirt, decked out in Dolce and Gabanna and Versace, with his slicked-back hair, incredible blue eyes and a smile that not only lit up his face but the whole room. (I know I mentioned his smile and eyes twice but they were that good that they needed two mentions!)

He told me he was a banker by day and a Royal Marine by night. That explains it. Royal Marine! Swooooon. I was heady already just at the thought of the uniform. We talked the rest of the night until closing time. When he was leaving, I walked with him to the door. He would not let go of my hand and nearly dragged me out of the club. I went home that night with a great big smile on my face.

The next day Matt called me at work and asked me on a date. We planned to meet in town and go for a pizza. I dressed cutely wearing a long black skirt with flower prints in lime and red and a little cropped lime chenille jumper. Matt was wearing khaki jeans and a baggy designer top. It seemed he had never been to Pizza Hut before and asked for chips, which made me giggle. He was strong and masculine but had an innocence that made me feel like a girl about town. That day I gave up my red meat ban, as he wanted a big pepperoni pizza, which we both rather enjoyed.

We then went off to the airport. In those days, you could go and have a drink in the airport and watch the flights taking off and landing. It had been a successful first date. A couple of days later, he came over for a meal, and I cooked him lamb bolognese. I was reluctant to eat beef as mad cow disease was still ongoing, and I figured I would use lamb instead. I had no idea of the culinary world and just put lamb, onions and Dolmio sauce together. It worked though, as he was impressed. Only ever having enough culinary skills to make himself pasta with corned beef and ketchup, my bolognese must have tasted heavenly.

Wendy came home and told me she had booked a holiday to Majorca and asked if I would like to come along. I had only been on holiday once before, to Tunisia, which was a bit intense. (I had no idea Tunisia was almost like Saudi. all I had taken were holiday clothes and got many an evil stare from the female locals at the morning market when I was parading around in my short shorts.) Wendy spoke Spanish as well as Italian, so it seemed a great idea to go on holiday with a girl, and she knew the island.

The departure date was soon upon us, and I was so excited. I had heard all about girl holidays, and Wendy was a bit of a party girl. We booked half board, so food wasn't an issue. The airport was busy. We lost ourselves in the heady mist of just about every scent in the duty-free shop, completely unaware that our name was being called, as we were late for boarding. We ran onto the plane to everyone`s tuts and eye rolls. As we walked to our seats, the plane was already pushing back. Phew!

We were off the plane and onto our coach. I was following Wendy`s lead as she knew what she was doing. The hotel was small and sweet in what was, at that time, a quiet resort called Sa Coma. I was introduced to sangria with our first evening meal, and everything seemed wonderful.

Next morning Wendy seemed a little down. She had started to see a Turkish guy two weeks before we came away. I think she had only seen him a couple of times, but she said she was missing him. He was a well-oiled, well-versed visa grabber if you ask me, but I had only met him once, and to me he did not seem very interested in Wendy. It was not my place to say anything, though.

She asked if we could go to the beach that day, not my ideal thing to do. I was hoping to explore, but maybe we could do that in the afternoon. The beach was beautiful but busy.

There were a lot of boobies around, and I hadn't expected that. I turned around to talk to Wendy just as she too was taking her top off. For being little and round, she had an enormous pair of boobs. Gosh, this was an eye-opener, so I did the same but remained on my front most of the time. It was the one, and only time I have dared to do that. Besides, they were much perkier then.

A random man kept going into the sea, then rolling himself in the sand in front of us, which was amusing to watch. I think it was either some weird mating ritual or a German way to exfoliate. Time was ticking by, and I was getting increasingly bored. We had walked past a Spanish supermarket on our way to the beach, and I said that I would like to have a look in on our way home, if that was OK. Wendy didn't say anything much.

We got melon for lunch from a vendor, and my skin was crisping up like streaky bacon under a hot grill. She made us stay at the beach all day. It seemed that was Wendy`s idea of a perfect holiday. Her holiday heaven was my holiday hell, with every day a carbon copy of the last, and with more crisping up until my skin was shedding. This, apparently, was what was supposed to happen. I looked like a very old threadbare patchwork quilt of brown and pink when I returned home.

We walked past the same supermarket every day on the way and return from the beach, and I stood opposite, wishing I could go in. Eating our evening meal in the hotel and a couple of sangrias before bed, Wendy moaned and moaned about her bloke. I ended up chatting to a couple who were at the hotel and spending time with them. I was grateful when it was time to leave.

Life returned to normal when we got home, except some money was missing from my bank account. My card had been in my drawer at home while I was away. It was only fifty pounds, but it was still very much accounted for. I have always been very careful and even now know where every penny is. My card had been used at a Metrocentre cash point the morning after we had returned from holiday. Mum had access to my house, which I guess meant my brother did too if he had stolen the key. But to be fair, I think he would have maxed me out not just taken fifty pounds.

I questioned my mum, but she denied it, and why would she go all the way to the Metrocentre when there were closer cashpoints in the local shopping centre? Wendy had been at work there that morning and had been complaining she was skint. I was a bit stupid in those days and had the same PIN number for everything. She could have easily got to know it.

A couple of weeks later, she moved out stating that she couldn't afford to live away from home anymore, although not before she trimmed my hair for me. I was booked to meet Matt's dad, and his family in Italy and Wendy said she was a qualified hairdresser. Blunt fringes were a la mode, and I fancied a change. I sat down with complete confidence and the vision of Naomi Campbell's new cut in my head. When she had finished, I went to look in the mirror and screamed in horror. OMG! She had cut me a blunt fringe all right, but it started at the back of the top of my head. She had then chopped into the sides of my hair and given me what can only be described as an '80s home-cut mullet on a hillbilly yokel. OMG! I was horrified, more than horrified, and my new boyfriend was at the door. He was sweet to me and said I looked cute. She had done it on purpose. It turned out she had been very jealous of me. Now I had to face Matt's family looking like a ten-year-old '80s throwback.

I don't even remember the flight to Italy. I had been sniffy, had taken an antihistamine, and it wiped me out completely. It's funny that the drowsy ones never have an effect, but the non-drowsy ones knock me out. Not the first or last time my body would be topsy-turvy.

Matt's dad, Salvatore, was very charming. He had a wife who spoke no English – Liliana. I could tell even then how much she loved his dad and what a kind and sweet lady she was. She couldn`t communicate with Matt verbally, but she loved him like a son all the same. She always bought him presents, did his washing and ironing and ran around after him, like any mum would when her boy was home.

Matt appreciated this greatly as his own mum was rubbish. She had come down with M.S. just after Matt's younger brother was born and she blamed Matt and Aaron, and anyone and everything. Bitterness was her middle name. A well-educated, well-spoken intelligent woman, fluent in Italian was Anne, or 'Katarina', as his dad called her. She let her illness consume her. She wanted pity from anyone that would listen. Very few people seemed to call her a friend as I think she had driven them in the same direction as Aaron's dad, which was right out of her life. The epitome of frugality, she made Scrooge look generous. She would not let Matt have lights on or heating. He had to sit in his coat in the house. She dished out toilet roll squares on request, one for a number one and two for a number two. She fed him mouldy food, as she would not waste anything. He had to ask for a drink of water. Everything was hers.

At one point, Matt's step-aunt threatened her with the social services as she was treating the boys so badly. Aaron knew no different, but Matt had known the kinder, softer mum she was when he was a young boy. He learned to switch off his emotions. If he didn't have any, then nothing could affect him. It took a long while to get through to him that the way she lived and helped him live was not normal. I was always just going to pull the toilet roll and wait until it stopped. It was my toilet roll – I paid for it. I was always going to have a warm house too. It took years and countless arguments to chip away out of him what she had ground in. Some people have children but have no idea how to be a parent. She was so bitter at Salvatore for leaving her that she punished Matt. He had never let anyone in except me and never had a girlfriend before me. After we eventually split up sixteen years later, he has not had one since. Jacob and I were his world, all that he needed.

Our trip to Italy had been fun. Matt managed to drop pomodoro sauce on his clean white T-shirt every day. He introduced me to the delights of Italian gelato (especially Nutella) and found a little bakery that sold focaccia col formaggio, which we could just about manage to order. We had a boat trip to Portofino, and I had taken my first expensive gadget with me. It was a camera that took pictures straight to floppy disk. It was fantastic, but it was the size and weight of a small TV.

The next month, in September, after just six months together, I asked Matt if he would like to move in with me. It seemed to be the right thing. We were massively in love. He got a lodger for his flat and moved in. Things were mostly great with Matt, apart from my trying to erase the damage his mother did to him. We lived side-by-side, going about our lives happily. Not being in each other's pockets, but giving enough room for the other to grow whilst knowing there was a pair of arms to hold you if you needed them. I didn't appreciate all that we had at that time. I guess I just went along with it. We were very compatible, with a mutual love of food that grew over the years, along with our bellies.

Chapter Seven

I changed job, as I had been headhunted by Specsavers in Newcastle. The fresh start sounded like a good idea, along with nine-to-five hours, something I had never done before. I started late in the year, but just a few weeks in, I got sick. It felt like a virus. I took a couple of weeks off, went back to work and got sick again. I was completely and utterly wiped out. I was eventually fired as I was no good to anyone, not even myself.

I have no idea why, but I went to a Chinese herbalist, a little, old guy who worked from his living room in Fenham, whom I found in the Yellow Pages, in the days before Google. He took my pulse, prodded me and got me to stick out my tongue. Then he said I had mild M.E and gave me a tea to drink. I wasn't even that sure what M.E was. I do remember that back in my mid-teens, I worked in a shoe shop in Scarborough. My best friend from school, Kate, had come in with her mum and sister. She told me Bert (Elizabeth) had M.E. I had looked at her and thought to myself, "But you look fine." That would come back to haunt me in the many years I've been sick myself. I often wondered if it was the Universe's way of playing a sick prank on me, or my own soul's way of judgement in the way of sufferance.

Goodness knows what was in that tea, but it sure was nauseating. I baulked at every sip of it. Six months later, though, I was back to work assessing insurance claims and selling diamonds at Beaverbrook's in the Metrocentre again. I never quite got back to my original strength though, and found I became sick much more easily than before. I never dreamt that one day the six months of fatigue would come back to haunt and blight me again.

Since being a little boy, Matt had always had a dream that one day he would live in a four-bedroom detached house with his family; that he would have stability and safety and would provide that for his loved ones. I had never had stability and security or a feeling of safety, so it seemed ideal to me too, but more of a pipe dream, as Matt loved to spend money. Without even knowing what he was doing, Matt was carefully manifesting his future, by holding a constant vision of what he wanted to come about in his life. Without desperation or asking for it, he just knew he would achieve it one day. This is something that today I totally believe in. Your thoughts are always creating, and it's very important to be mindful of what you think. I'm sure there will be some more examples along the way, but here is the first one I ever recall.

One of our favourite things to do was to look at new housing developments. This went along with Matt's dream, but was also a great way to get style tips for home decoration. The green stripy sofa I had owned before showed I had terrible taste. Two years in, we came across a development at the Royal Quays. It was all being redeveloped after the Meadow Well riots many years before. We had been shopping over that way at the retail outlet. It was right by the river Tyne and looked lovely.

The show home was a semi, two bed on one side and three on the other. Both looked pretty but small, as happens in new homes. The salesman asked if we liked them, and Matt said we did but were looking for something bigger, which made me chuckle but feel nervous too. We didn't have two pennies to rub together and were a few grand in debt to boot. The man was very kind and said there was one at the end of the road, and gave us the key. The house style was a 'Dory,' made by Bellway. Walking down, it looked amazing. The way it was positioned on the street made it look imposing, and the front faced out onto the marina and right down the River Tyne.

Oh my goodness, this was something I could not have wished for even in my wildest dreams. I laid on the bedroom floor and said this is where our bed would be. I went in every room and imagined how we would live. Every bit of the house was designed to maximise space - it was perfect. The house was a bargain, but sadly, we just didn't have any money. With great reluctance, we gave the key back and went home. A few weeks later, it had been sold, and it felt wrong to see other people's things in our house and a strange car on our drive.

We would often talk about and visit the Dory, calling it "Our house," we would sit and admire the view and imagine we were in the house. It all sounds pathetic, doesn't it? It probably was, that is, until the beginning of 1999. We were getting married in the April (My dad was going to give us some money towards the wedding, one of the only good things he did), and we had a little visit to our house on the way to buy some wedding stuff.

As we pulled up, we saw it looked empty. It was for sale again. Now this was great news, but on the other hand, we were in an even less favourable position financially, as Matt had decided to buy a car the size of a stretch limo. We still had no money and lots of debt. Nevertheless, Matt let curiosity get the better of him, and he rang the estate agent.

The house had been part-exchanged with a builder in Leeds, as the owners had relocated due to work. The builder wanted it off his hands, and Matt asked if he would consider part-exchanging his own flat. I wondered where all this was going, as both our houses were in a stalemate position, if not negative equity, with no money for any fees, let alone a removal man. The builder agreed to consider this, depending on the valuation.

Well, blow me down! It turned out that someone, it seemed, was looking out for us. Matt was offered just enough money for the house to cover his mortgage and the associated fees for selling and buying. The bank agreed to lend us exactly what we wanted, but we were maxed-out to the penny. This was really going to happen. All those years of believing and calling that home our own had paid off. We had no idea what we were doing at the time, but we manifested that house to be ours. We created it and made it reality. It still took work and belief, but it did work. I know now of the strength we have as energy beings, creative beings, but I did not know how we had gotten it back then. I figured it had just been a fluke.

We moved into our dream home on March 25th 1999, and married on April 6th. It was perfect. We had hardly any furniture to fill a house like that. Ironically, we had been to Ikea before we got the house and had chosen some wardrobes that we loved. Lo and behold, when we got inside the house, the exact wardrobes were there, ready built and left by the previous owners, as they didn't have room for them. What a divine gift. It almost felt like magic.

By this time, my middle brother was somewhat of a lost cause. Whilst I lived in my little house, he had been in and out of living with Mum, who was only a mile up the road (she had moved to be closer to me and to try and escape him a couple years before, but he followed her). People's houses around the area were being burgled. Mum had just got a new pay-per-view TV, (one of those huge, heavy things), with the promise that both boys were going to help put the money in it to keep it running.

One day while she was out, the TV disappeared along with the full coin box. It was strange, because there were minimal signs of a break-in. The rest of the things she held dear were gone too, although she had managed to hide and therefore keep hold of little rings and necklaces. He had managed to take everything she had ever owned that had some street value, even if it were pennies. Of course, he denied it until the cows came home, but it had him all over it. There were rumours he was behind all the other burglaries too.

I later found out that my old boyfriend, Mark, had been arrested for criminal activities around this time. Only when the police looked into the description of the 'Mark' they arrested did they realise somebody had given the wrong name and address as a deterrent. It took him some time and going to court to erase that from his otherwise clean record. They only had to look at him to realise that he was not six-foot-one with tattoos! We certainly know who fit that description and who would have known Mark's details. He also stole Mark's prized watch that he had been given for his twenty-first birthday, another thing I had to replace with my own money.

On another occasion, again around the same time as the watch, (how I wish he hadn't known where I lived) he turned up on my doorstep. He had been working as a security guard. Instead of doing his job, he spent the nights ringing up chat lines to the cost of £1000. There he was on his knees in tears outside my door begging me to help him. Some people were going to kneecap him or worse, he said. Please, please, please lend me the money. I swear I will pay every penny back. I refused over and over again, but he would not leave. It wasn't the first or last time he would use this tactic. In the end, I felt I had little choice. I went to the bank and took out a loan. He never paid a penny of the loan or the interest I had to pay. Then came the car. Somehow he managed to get a car, financed with the backing of my mum. Were they serious? They took a middle-aged lady on benefits as a guarantor to a guy with a shocking credit history, who had only had a job for a few weeks?

The car lasted a couple of weeks before it disappeared, which was probably a good thing, as he had learned to drive in the TWOC (taken without consent) school of motoring. I am almost sure he had never passed a proper test, so therefore was also uninsured. It was a disaster waiting to happen. When he sold the car off illegally, it was left to my poor old mum to foot the bill, and I have no idea how she managed that.

Needless to say, a couple of years later, she went bankrupt owing £18,000, and that wasn't including the £2000 I found out she owed on a credit card in my name she had picked up from my letterbox. I don't have any ill will against my mum. At that time, she was robbing Peter to pay Paul, and most of it was due to my brother. She was also suffering from misdiagnosed Crohn's disease, which all this stress didn't help. Her idea was to take the NHS to court for negligence, as they had messed up a varicose vein operation and left her in permanent pain. The solicitor reckoned she would get around 18k, so she counted on that to bail her out. The doctor who was supporting her case then pulled out.

She started with one credit card but couldn't keep up with repayments, so she got another one and took cash out to pay the first. She didn't have 18k of gold watches and luxury purchases lying around. If she wasn't paying another card, her food bill went on there, plus the interest on the interest. Neither of the boys was bringing in money, and she was clothing, feeding and giving money to both. She was just silly with money, my mum, a soft, kind-hearted person. She didn't mean for it to get out of control. The stress brought on the Crohn's Disease, so she had a lot of karma that came back to her, bless her.

Once at my new address, I strictly told my mum not to tell my middle brother where I lived. I even threatened her with my never seeing her again if he found out. She was not even allowed to write it down. My little brother was also threatened with the pain of death, but he was so much into internet dating by that time that his head was not away from his computer long enough to have any conversation with anyone. He was never told my address, right up until the last of year of Mum's life.

My deeply troubled sandy-haired brother with a smile so wide and bright would disappear for quite a while. Sometimes it was because he was in jail, having served more than once at Frankland Prison. Twice I believe he was found nearly dead of a heroin overdose on the streets of Edinburgh. He didn't know how to survive without drugs and crime, as doing an honest day's work and paying bills didn't make sense to him.

There came the point about a year before Mum died that my brother was clean. I had had nothing to do with him for years, which was my choice. I had had too many nights crying, wondering what was happening to him and feeling guilty for breathing fresh air and walking down the street when he was locked up. I felt guilty for making the right choices and being happy. While he was clean and determined to stay clean, it seemed only right to give him a chance.

We organised a little flat for him somewhere between Mum's house and mine. Matt and I furnished it as best we could with a sofa, bed, small TV and kitchen stuff. He seemed to be OK. Mum gave him food parcels. We all kept an eye on him. He didn't seem to manage his dole money well and thought he could have Sky TV and a top phone contract yet never buy anything to eat!

He had started to say that there were dodgy people around where he lived and that he kept seeing the same car sitting outside his home. Then people were following him. It all started to put us on high alert. It was suspected he was taking drugs again, which was something he strongly denied. Matt, being the cop he is, went round to his flat and found that it was trashed. My brother had slashed open the couch and the bed mattress looking for recording devices. The TV and everything that could be was taken apart, again looking for bugs.

He had tried to poison Mum, and she wouldn't let him in the house, so he came to the back window one day, asking for a hot drink. Mum put her cup down and turned round to put the kettle back on only to find her tea was fizzing when she picked it back up. She too was under suspicion as he thought she was in on the whole conspiracy to kill him. He was so paranoid. Once he was found in a Tesco car park shouting that the security guards were after him, and running around with a bag of hammers and knives he had stolen from Mum and other places.

In the end, I forced Mum to get him sectioned. He had been taking quite big doses of amphetamines, and they had given him psychosis. Finally, after all the abuse he had given his body, his brain gave up. He was transferred to a lockdown facility was accompanied day and night by a carer. However, he still managed to escape through a toilet window the size of a matchbox.

He was on the run for a little while, but without his psychosis meds, he got into trouble and went back to the facility. He was slowly allowed access to the normal world, but he always seemed to mess things up. I saw him on the day of Mum's funeral in 2008 accompanied by a carer (he still managed to steal my friend's purse, which we found in his jacket pocket) I've not heard a word since. I don't know if he is dead or alive. For my own sake, it is better that way as I can't take responsibility for him. Rick had done so for a while after Mum passed but moved when his second child was born, and it was reported that our brother had been dealing drugs in the West End of Newcastle. I still feel some guilt to this day when I think about him. Where is he? What is he doing? But I guess I know the answer. I feel guilty for being normal, for making the right choices, and also feeling guilty that he didn't. We had both had the same childhood after all.

So back to Matt, myself, and our happy home. We were going to move in on February 25th and get married on April 6th, which was a lot to plan, so Matt organised the move, and I organised the wedding. All was going fantastically until Matt's 'friends' organised his stag do. They all loved clubbing, so had decided to go to Tall Trees in Yarm, with the start of the night in Middlesbrough. They had planned to stay overnight, which was understandable as it was a long way for a taxi.

At 2 a.m, the key went in the front door, and I rushed downstairs to find Matt staggering in. He had a lift home in a taxi with his well-off friend, as he said he didn't want to stay out. Fair enough, I thought, as he staggered off to the loo. He was gone for a while, so I went to make sure he hadn't fallen in, only to find him sitting on the loo with his white underpants around his ankles, but a very visible smear all over them jumped out at me. It was ladies' foundation caked all over the front of them. I don't wear any base makeup but know many women do. Immediately I was in self-defence mode.

"What the f*** is that?" (I am always someone who doesn't swear unless I am backed into a corner, then I know plenty of expletives) Oh my! It was all making sense. He was home because of guilt. He muttered, "I can explain," he wasn't even aware that his encounter had left its tell-tale marks. As I marched him to bed, he mumbled a story that didn't make sense. I was due to go to work, but that night had little sleep.

I decided to lock him in and take his house and car keys with me to work, along with the home telephone (no mobiles in those days). I needed to find out what happened before he had time to collaborate a story with those scumbag boys. My friend Sue who I got the bus with found it hilarious as I recalled the tale and sat there with the huge home phone on my lap.

Later that day, I rang Alan's wife Susan and got the story from him (he hadn't even turned up home until much later the next day). The story went that they were in a pub when a tarty, not very pretty, "stripper," organised by his so-called mates, came in. I'm not prudish and figured that would probably happen. This woman however was not a stripper but a prostitute. She stripped off her clothes and writhed around on Matt, which I am sure they were all enjoying. She then started to unbutton his trousers and rub her face in his groin. At that point, he pointed out his desperate friend who never got any girls, so she moved on and gave her special paid-for favour to him. Matt, at that point, realised he just wanted to go home.

I am all for a bit of fun, but to pay for a last night of sex for a man who is getting married? What kind of person did they think Matt was? It showed how much they thought of me! They were immediately uninvited to our wedding. It is just a good job I didn't drive, as I would have gone straight over to them and given them a piece of my mind and probably a punch in the face.

It wasn't a grand affair, my big day. My dad had said he would pay towards it and I knew Tracey had had quite a big wedding the £20k type. My dad thought I was only after his money and that I wouldn't want to know him if he had been a dustman, which of course was ridiculous. I would rather he be poor and humble. So we opted for a low key, informal type wedding at a nice hotel, the Gosforth Park. It was a small gathering of close family and friends followed by food and then an evening do with some more friends.

I had two bridesmaids, Karen and Allison, and Karen's niece Nicola as a flower girl. It was beautiful. Neither of us were religious, and I knew that I didn't have to get married in a church to prove anything to anyone. I walked down the little aisle to the beautiful harp and voice of Janet, and it felt magical. I was told I looked like a Grecian goddess. I'm not sure about that, but I loved my dress, which was straight and a little beading on the bodice. It was perfectly understated.

I chose not to have speeches. Why would I? My mum was the only person who really knew me. My dad didn't know me, but he was paying towards it, so I didn't feel it was right for my mum to speak, or my dad. It made it less formal, and I liked that. There was only one problem. My dad said I didn't make him feel important enough, so he initially refused to pay the hotel bill. Even on my wedding day, he wanted to make it about him.

Matt's dad and Liliana paid for our honeymoon. I think there was a little bit of competition with who could do the best in the 'Dad' stakes. He gave us £3000 for our trip. We settled on Margarita Island, Venezuela. I had been all the way around the world in my search for the perfect place. I didn't want to do the conventional places. Margarita was the last Caribbean Island in the chain of islands and sounded exotic.

Just a few days before we were to set off, we got notice that they had changed the flight times. We were going to miss half of our wedding reception, so no honeymoon suite but instead a taxi journey through the wee hours to Manchester with a driver who kept falling asleep. We had a little picnic of our wedding buffet food for our time in the airport. It was very sweet. I was just glad to get there in one piece. I talked to the driver constantly to try to keep him awake.

I don't remember the plane journey, but I remember the transfer, arriving at a beautiful hotel and being welcomed with drinks. Our room was so big it had two king-size beds in it, but it did smell damp. We figured the smell was coming from the air conditioner unit, and it was due to the humidity. We were so tired from travelling we wandered down to the beach lay on some sunbeds and fell asleep. As the sun dropped in the sky, it burned my scalp where my parting was. It hurt all week.

Margarita was a beautiful island, but one of those places you are not encouraged to go out of the resort. We wandered around only to find an armed guard by the beach, and most of it covered in dead fish the next day, as if there had been an explosion in the sea. Life was an endless round of chargrilled chicken from the barbeque bar, cocktails and lots of other lovely food. That was until I spent the second week constantly on the toilet! I was the only person that could come back from two weeks all-inclusive holiday having lost weight. Matt was unaffected. He had eaten so much bacteria as a child that he was immune.

We took a taxi one day into the main city of Porlamar, which was busy and scary. I don't think we were there long as there was just an uneasy feeling in the air. On another day, we went on an organised small yacht trip. Matt turned an awful shade of green and spent the outbound journey with his head over the back of the boat. I found my sea legs and helped make the sandwiches. We snorkelled in some beautiful shallow water where I gashed my knee, then sailed off back to shore.

On the way back, the coach stopped at a souvenir shop in the middle of nowhere where there was a toilet too. The locals in their doorless and windowless shacks stood and watched all the foreigners waiting for the loo. I think this was their pastime. It was a poor island and a far cry from the luxury of the resort we were in. It was the first time I had seen that divide outside of Saudi Arabia.

We got talking to other people on holiday too, particularly a couple with two children. They were on the same flight home as us. The children seemed to attach themselves to us, and we spent most of the eleven-hour flight with them on our knees. Matt seemed natural around kids, which was lovely to see given his own difficult childhood.

Once we landed on terra firma, we were back to our new beautiful home, and we settled into married life well, buying bits and pieces as we could and making our little nest. I was young and still had very little in the way of good taste. Over the years, those walls were painted a variety of colours, with me deciding one day even to go Greek in the hallway. I made a brick shape out of a sponge and painted a sky blue brick wall about two feet tall along the hallway and up the stairs on the otherwise white walls. Needless to say, that didn't stay there long.

Another time, Matt came home to find I had painted the en-suite bathroom cerise pink, and all the accessories that were previously gold were now silver. The next day I decided I no longer liked it and left poor Matt to repaint it and scrape all the silver off the accessories, which he did, bless him. He was great at letting me follow my whims, even when he knew they would be a disaster. I think looking back in hindsight I probably didn't realise how great he really was. I've always been such a perfectionist and find it easy to pick at the small things but not see the bigger picture.

Every day I walked the mile through the park to the metro train station singing, skipping and talking to the birds and the trees. As tired as I was, I was always annoyingly happy on a morning. The world always seemed a wonderful, magical place, and I was just so happy to be part of it. I would bound into work with a huge grin on my face.

I had started a new job about a year into my marriage. My friend Alison had started working at an upmarket jeweller in Eldon Square, and they were looking for another staff member to do all their books. They were turning from predominantly paper filed records to a computerised system. I was to learn the new system and train everyone else. Two weeks in and I was wondering what I was doing there. It was the most pretentious place, because people who shopped there had serious money. I was glad I was mostly out the back, as I never could stand people who spoke in false posh voices and brown-nosed.

One day the computer software man came in to talk to me and show me the new package, so I sat all day listening and learning. At the end of the day, I tried to get up out of my chair and felt all dizzy and wobbly. At the time, I figured I had been sitting under an air-conditioning vent all day and just got a chill when I felt the warmer air hit me. The next morning I was feeling unwell, as if I had a virus, so I called in sick. I felt awful about this, as I hadn't been there long. The aches and pains seemed to move around my body over the next days and weeks. When my kidney felt unwell, then my brain would feel all fluey and foggy, then my tummy would be upset. One area after another, then back to the first. I just couldn't seem to shake it and was so fatigued. I'm not sure how long it was that I didn't bathe, but I wasn't smelling fresh. Matt helped as much as he could, bless him.

After a couple of weeks, I eventually got the sack. I'd been sick more than I had worked there.

With finances maxed out for our new home, I was feeling not only guilty but freaked out. Matt's wage wasn't enough, and I had to get myself well as soon as possible. The next few weeks passed in a sleepy, completely worn-out blur. I slept and slept but just could not seem to shake this virus. I eventually ended up going to see my GP, who did a range of bloods etc. No markers came back in the bloods, but he told me he thought I had M.E.

At that moment, the world suddenly went silent and stopped turning. The little Chinese herbal man had given me this same diagnosis those few years ago. I went home and back to my bed, not knowing what to think. Matt assured me it would be OK, and that last time I was back on my feet within six months. I agreed with him and said I would use Chinese medicine again, hoping that it would help once more. I dared not tell him that this felt different, as I had this sense that it was far more serious than before. I didn't know where that sense came from and brushed it aside.

Once I came to terms with the diagnosis, I set about fixing it once again. The little old guy was no longer available, so I found one of the new type of high street Chinese medicine shops. I gave the man my symptoms, and he felt a few places, looked at my tongue, and surprisingly came up with the same diagnosis. I signed up for his recommended and very expensive course of acupuncture, massage and medicine.

I was shown to a little room with a massage bed, and then the Chinese doctor came in. He was just a young person with a sweet accent and very kind eyes. He explained what he was going to do and set about tapping needles into my face. It wasn't painful in itself, just a very weird feeling. They were left in for a while, and then he removed them. I quite liked it, and it felt almost cleansing. He then told me to turn over, whereupon he gave me what can only be described as a martial arts massage. Blimey, I felt like I had gone several rounds with Jackie Chan. Anyone would feel better once that stopped! He gave me a tea to drink and off I went. The tea had a similar taste to the one a few years before, but there was definitely something missing, in that it wasn't as putrid, probably missing rhino testicles or elephants penis. I have no idea what was in it, but it still tasted vile.

The ME still hasn't gone, twenty years later. As I sit and write this, it is still very much present every day, every second to be exact. The early days were filled with a sense of hope that it would be a short-lived thing. I guess it made it easier to cope with, thinking it was going to go eventually. It never entered my mindset that I wouldn't return to work; that my life would never be the same again or that the once effervescent person full of energy and life would never be seen again.

Well, I guess that's not really the right thing to say. She is still very much there, even today. That person is still in my head and my heart, even though my thought processes feel like I am wading through toffee. However, I still have the positivity and enthusiasm for life, although my energy level rarely if ever allows me to take part in it. There are glimpses at times, when I've pushed myself to extremes and for just a very short while I've been able to blag it. No one would know from looking at me, even twenty years later.

I have tried hard to keep my trim figure, as I always was good at eating healthily, although I love food. I love a massive pile of mixed, chopped everything in the fridge salad – for example – with feta, ham and apple included, sprinkled with chopped dry-roasted nuts for some extra texture.

Those early days were difficult. It was like pulling things from thin air. After all the bills were paid, we were left with £25 a week food money and £25 a week to buy everything else, such as toiletries, clothes, treats and emergencies and to live on.

Luckily, we lived a short drive from a great wholesale fruit and veg place. £10 would get you a huge Ikea blue bag full of fruit and veg for the week. I bought whatever was cheapest too and tried to make things around those ingredients.

With the illness, I had to think seriously about cooking. It had to be quick, as I couldn't stand for long, and on a budget. On the way home from the wholesalers was a cheap butcher who sold 5lb of lamb steaks or rump steaks for a fiver, so we always got those too. BOGOF offers had just started at the supermarkets, back in the days when they truly meant 'buy one get one free'. We lived well on our little bit of money.

Chapter Eight

I had never been much of a maternal person. I had accepted this when I had been pregnant at twenty-one. I don't think I'd even thought of the wider implications of it all. After what happened, I had written off any chance of having a child. The last thing I needed to do was lose my last remaining kidney. That's serious, right? So I didn't think about it at all. Then I found myself forced to be at home poorly, married and wondering what was going on in my life.

Talking with Matt, we concluded that if we were ever to try for a baby, it would be now and only now. I could rest for the whole time. Health problems meant I could not work, so maybe this was a sign. Yeah, maybe back then I did believe in signs although I probably took very little notice of most of them.

Matt had worked lots of overtime, bless him, so that we could afford a little holiday, back in the day when you could go away for around £99 each. St George in the south of Crete is a tiny little fishing village down a very steep hill. Thank God, it was night-time when the crazy Greek driver got us there. In the daytime, we saw how dangerous the road was. We were booked into a tiny family-run B&B called "Phaistos." The plug sockets and light switches were hanging off the walls. There were mildewed shower curtain and tiles as well as a smell of damp. But it was clean, basic but clean. That's all we could ask for £99.

The little old lady who ran it was a bit like the Godfather, with short hair, tiny build and dressed in black. She seemed to be everywhere we went, with fingers in all the pies of the little fishing village. If she liked you, there were boiled eggs at breakfast. We got a bread bun and a bit of jam, and I think she even begrudged us the jam. We found an amazing little restaurant called "Madame Hortense." It served arni kleftiko, which was lamb wrapped in filo pastry. Wow, we had it three times in a week.

This holiday was our relaxation and de-stressing time – well, more for Matt, as my life had become a lot less stressful, not being able to do much. We decided this was where we would try to make a baby. So we did, the night before we left to go home.

The next morning we were sorted and ready to go home and waited for our coach from the bar next door. We ordered a cold coke and sat down at a table to get the last few rays of the sun. They had the big screen TV on the news channel, and everyone seemed to be gathering around it. I glanced over to see the horrifying blood-curdling sight of the second plane going into the Twin Towers in New York. OMG, as it all unfurled in disbelief on the screen, words scrolling underneath that this was the second tower hit.

Then the towers fell.

We all sat there, shocked beyond belief. The words 'terrorists' and 'hijacking' were being used. It suddenly dawned on me that we were sitting waiting to go to the airport to get onto an aeroplane. Time seemed to go somehow slower than normal. There were motions, getting onto the bus, off at the airport, looking around to see who was getting on our flight, were there any strange looking people? It was a dizzy mix of adrenaline and fear, knowing we had to go home and hoping that it would be an uneventful flight.

It was as if the Universe felt the effects of those attacks that day. There was thunder and lightning nearly all the way home, turbulence making the flight feel like a rollercoaster, lightning bolts striking just beyond the tips of the wings putting everyone on high alert. It was one of the most bizarre days of my life, but everyone rallied together. We all spoke to each other. People who you would have more or less ignored on a regular day became instantly friendly. I guess it was a combination of 'Britishness', of rallying together and stiff upper lips, with the shock that everyone felt. A day very few people of the world will forget. When the aeroplane landed every passenger clapped and cheered, we were just thankful to have got back to the UK safely.

Within a couple of weeks of being home, I started to feel sick. Instantly I knew there was a life growing inside of me. The nausea got worse to the point that I couldn't eat or even sip water. I was hospitalized with hyperemesis and given some medication. The doctors reassured me this level of nausea indicated a healthy pregnancy, and they even wanted to check to see if it was twins.

That day I was able to see my baby for the very first time. It was a tiny bean, but it was mine, and I felt such a bond with that little being. From that day onwards, I started talking to him. I just knew it was a boy. Something inside me just knew. I also knew that he was going to be called Jacob. It was a good job that Matt liked that name, as there was not even a discussion about an alternative. My days consisted of resting and trying to eat and drink. Matt would do the dutiful thing and get me anything I wanted (which was very little), but he usually ended up eating it. At around twenty weeks, the nausea eased off, and I could settle into my pregnancy.

We had decided to have a little break and booked ourselves on the DFDS ferry going to Amsterdam, as it departed from very near where we lived. We booked a cute little room quite high up on the ship, stood out on the deck as we left the mouth of the Tyne, having a cuddle and having a Titanic moment. It was romantic.

That was until the ferry started bobbing up and down in the ocean current and we scurried back inside.

Dinner was a smorgasbord of all delights, eating as much as we dared on an undulating ship, followed by drinks in the bar and a surprisingly good night sleep. Waking in the morning, we ate a breakfast buffet as we pulled into the harbour in Holland. A bus took us into the centre of Amsterdam where we walked for a few hours, eating the local delicacy of chips and mayonnaise (continental mayonnaise is just the best). Stumbling across the red light district, we giggled at the sights in the windows. Then finally, we found the Anne Frank Museum, which was surprisingly tiny and a real window into the events that unfolded for all those poor people.

Back on board, we settled down with some sandwiches as we sailed down-river. It had been a lovely little trip. Not long after setting off, the boat started to undulate more and more. We were hitting some stormy weather. With the ship listing from side to side, the waves were coming up over the top of the boat and being in a high room meant we were swinging about like a chandelier. That familiar feeling started welling up inside my stomach so much so that I knew I was going to be sick. I got up to wobble to the toilet when Matt rushed past me and got there first. I headed for the sink. It wasn't very pleasant as I have always vomited noisily. I soon discovered that it actually felt much better if I lay down as I was not bobbing about as much. I didn't get out of my clothes that night. I figured if we were going down, it wasn't with my nightie on! I was worried that the little portable TV was going to fall on me too. Sleep was not something we had that night.

My baby bump was growing nicely. I could feel him moving around, and at the next scan, it was confirmed that baby was indeed a boy. I couldn't have asked for a better baby. When I was tired, I told him we needed to sleep, and he stayed quiet and still and when I ate he got very excited. I had read that if you eat spicy or garlicky food, the flavours transfer through to the amniotic fluid and make the baby less fussy. So I ate as flavourful a diet as I could.

Every week our treat was to go to Chinatown in Newcastle and have a lunchtime special menu, always starting with hot and sour soup. Within seconds of eating it, Jacob would start to move around, every single time. I don't know if it was because I was excited to eat it and he felt that, but by the time he was born and one-and-a-half years old he was sitting at the table eating his own hot and sour soup, much to the amazement of other eaters in the restaurant. Food it seemed was a theme even before he came out! A typical Bruno. They are a family of big appetites.

I was monitored quite closely because of my kidney disease and the fact of the M.E. By thirty-eight weeks, they had decided I was too exhausted and didn't want to risk my kidney any further, so I was taken in for an induction. Several pills and pokes later, he still wasn't convinced he should come out. The doctor recommended an epidural. Ouch, that hurt going in! But it meant I sat for sixteen hours with Matt feeding me ice cubes and felt nothing at all. However, this also meant that Jacob was incredibly relaxed and not bothered at all to get himself out.

One last chance before an emergency C-section was the ventouse cap. I heard a very loud pop (which turned out to be my bits splitting, ouch) and out he came. They laid this tiny little mousey-haired boy on my chest. I felt overwhelmed with love. He had grey eyes, a fringe at the back of his hair and a face that looked like it had been pressed up against a sweet shop window for too long. He looked up at me without making a sound and then did a wee all over me. Welcome to the world, Jacob Bailey Bruno.

In those first few weeks, the mousey hair and long back fringe all fell out and left just a few short strands of blonde hair, just as I had been as a baby. Those slate grey eyes turned crystal-clear blue and that wrinkly face straightened out. What a beautiful little boy.

It was very clear where his nose came from right from day one. That pudgy squishy nose was definitely Matt's. He was like an amalgamation of both of us, bits of me and bits of Matt combined with his own unique bits. Perfection!

From the moment he came home, he went straight into his own room and his own cot. Peace of mind was given to us by an angel care monitor (a mat that detects breathing and makes a beep through a monitor). With the help of a regular routine and baby lavender baths, within a few weeks he was sleeping right through.

He was so hungry by six weeks that even hungrier baby formula didn't satisfy him, I took him to the doctors and told him that every time we ate he nearly bounced himself out of his low chair and made eating faces. The doctor said just to feed him then, as one of his own children had been the same. So at six weeks of age, Jacob started on his eating adventure. Boy, did that kid love his food!

Apart from falling asleep headfirst in his first Christmas dinner, he was amazing. By the time of his first birthday party, he was well versed. I made all of his favourite things that day, for him and a few close friends, such as beef lasagne, mild chilli with three kinds of beans, and a curry. We also had a BBQ with gyros and tzatziki, which he loved too. This was a mini eating machine. He would happily try anything, and there was very little he didn't like (e.g. raw onions, but will eat them cooked in food) and off the top of my head, still to this day I can't make a list, although he would always prefer home-cooked food to ready-prepared meals. At one point around the age of eight, he decided he would be a food critic when he grew up. Then he started critiquing my food which quickly got stopped with my saying, "Right, I'm not cooking anymore. I am going on strike." That soon sorted that one out.

Food was not the only thing that came very natural to Ja. He almost came out talking. He was desperate to talk and tried his best to communicate in all ways. He seemed to miss big steps, went from sitting to standing, bypassing the whole crawling around stage. He went from garble to speech easily too. The toilet was the same. One day he decided he did not want to sit on the big, blue teddy bear potty I had bought for the downstairs toilet. He used it just a few times, then he saw what we did and wanted to do the same. Being so small was perilous. He fell in the toilet several times, even with a child seat extension on it. Poor kid, he was desperate to be a grown-up. I always knew there was something unique about him, though. He just seemed connected to me in a way I had not seen in other children.

Then one day, it became clear. Even before he had come to grips with full sentences –

so somewhere around one-year-old – I was riding in the back of the car with him. I had a migraine (this was quite common. the M.E seemed to trigger that response in me). I was sitting there, swaying about with the car thinking to myself, 'Don't be sick, don't be sick,' when Ja looked at me very clearly and said, "Don't be sick." This was a little baby who didn't even know what 'don't be sick' meant! He had never been sickly. Once he had the food in him, he wasn't going to give it back. I hadn't said a thing out loud, so the only way he could have repeated what I had said in my own head was that he was able to read my thoughts.

Over the next few weeks, this happened several times. Each time it blew me away. I now know that this is something all babies do. In vitro the baby has telepathic communication with its mum. One of the big reasons why a stressed parent has a stressed baby is that the baby is subjected to stress in the body and the mental and emotional anguish, too. I became massively aware of the actual impact the mother has on her growing foetus and how that translates to what kind of baby she has. I am no doctor, but I am a mother and a sensitive. Science does not know everything. It is constantly re-evaluating and disproving itself. I wish all mothers knew the real impact that they have on their baby and how much easier things could be for many mothers if they would take time to recognise that.

Babies are souls just as adults are. They have just gone the full circle completed their last life, had a little rest and then moved to their next body and next set of lessons. They are not the empty vessels many people think they are. Children are wise. They don't have the prejudices that adults do. They are almost reset back to the pure spirit self that we all are without our physical body shell, memories of the previous life and the way of the Universe carefully stored so they can live this next set of lessons.

The more of these lives we have, the thinner that wall we have created between this physical life and those stored memories. It's all there within each of us, but some of us have a clearer access than others. Those delicate things most of us ignore. Those gut feelings, those instincts are our most valuable senses. There are more people than ever in the world coming to realise this and bringing themselves to be better in tune with these, but we still have a long way to go. We are still far behind the advanced civilisations that have come and gone a long time before us.

Chapter Nine

Soon Jacob was moving around by himself and exploring, and little weird things started to happen. I was upstairs with Matt when I heard a loud noise of something falling onto the floor downstairs. I ran down to see what it was and a small book that I had put on the windowsill earlier was lying in the middle of the floor. No windows were open, and nobody was downstairs.

We had a small hamster at the time. Jacob called her 'Cookie'. No matter how much we tied her door to her cage, we would find her wandering about on her own. I started sensing that someone else was in the room. I don't know how or why I knew, but I felt that there was a boy. I hadn't told anyone but Matt, but Jacob came up to me one day and told me there was a boy in the room. He started to refer regularly to this boy. It seemed very normal to him, but he seemed not to like him too much.

One night when we had gone to bed, we heard a sound coming from Jacob's room. Fearing he was up playing and out of his cot, Matt sneaked in to see Jacob fast asleep and his remote control toy car moving across the room. Clearly the result of duff batteries. So Matt removed them from the car and the controller. He climbed back into bed, and as we were dropping off to sleep, we heard the same sound of the car moving again. I think it was the next day when Jacob mentioned the boy again and said he didn't like that boy. I asked why, out of curiosity, and he replied, "Because he plays with my toys." I had to laugh.

We had decided to treat ourselves to a new bed and had to get rid of the old one. While waiting for the delivery date, we slept in the spare room at the back of the house. This room had the upstairs BT phone socket but not enough space for the computer desk, which was in the third bedroom at the front. In the days before WIFI and laptops, it was common to have a cable going from your socket to your computer, which in this case ran across the bedroom laminate floor and into the other bedroom.

On this particular night, Matt was home, and we were tucked up in bed. Just as we were dropping off to sleep, we heard a tapping sound. It sounded like the telephone wire being tapped on the laminate floor. We thought it weird and checked just to make sure Cookie the hamster hadn't escaped again, but she was busy stuffing her face with seeds. Matt got back into bed, and it went quiet.

Suddenly a hand grabbed the wire on the floor and picked it up. It was obviously a hand because you could hear the fingernails scrape along the laminate. Both Matt and I jumped up and swore, as it was such a shock. We both looked at each other and couldn't even laugh as it had sounded so creepy.

Weird things now seemed to be happening quite often. The next night, Matt was on shift, and I went to the spare room on my own. There was no tapping, so I was grateful for that, but as I was drifting off to sleep, I opened my eyes and saw a head moving across the room. What on earth? It looked like the Medusa mythical figure, with snakes for hair. I wasn't scared at all but just thought it very unusual and watched as it moved around. It didn't seem to be solid, but it was very detailed. Then within about fifteen seconds, it dissipated. What was that all about, I asked myself? Then the answer came to me as clear as day. It was a symbol of change, and new things were coming fast. I accepted the information and went to sleep. I didn't expect the life-changing path that was to come.

I had been praying every night since I became pregnant. This carried on after I gave birth. It felt right to be thankful for the amazing opportunities that we had. Once I was aware of this little spirit boy, I would include him in my prayers too. I would send love to him, and every night without fail as I did this, my head would start spinning as if I'd just come off the Waltzer at the fair. It felt like my soul was being 'pulled'.

My aunt Sue (Dad's sister), who I had just met, had come up for a visit with my cousin

Tania. They were both sensitives too, and had apparently opened up to it all at the same time I had, without any of us knowing each other. As we were sitting, talking spiritual stuff and guides, she mentioned this little boy, said that he was my boy from a past life, who wanted to come to me in this life, and was jealous that I had a different little boy now. This totally made sense and in some way, I had felt he had been mine. The pulling at me when I sent him love made me think he had a big attachment to me. It wasn't long after this that Jacob came toddling into my bedroom. I was sitting on the loo in the en-suite. "Mama, there is a doctor over there," he said. I asked him why there was a doctor. "He said the little boy needs a doctor because he lives here".

That night the weirdest thing happened. Matt was on late shift, and I had put Jacob to bed and was sitting relaxing and watching TV. I can remember the programme on C4. It was about celebrities getting prosthetic makeovers and trying to fool their friends and family. The programme had just started a break when I looked at my mobile phone to see what time it was. 10.38 pm. I looked back up to the TV to see the next programme start. I chuckled to myself, and thought, "Stupid C4, how can it miss the end of a programme out?" When I looked back at my phone again, it was after 11 pm! Literally, seconds had passed between looking at my phone, looking back at the TV, then looking at my phone again.

I sat questioning what had happened. Had I fallen asleep? I wasn't someone who falls asleep in front of the TV. Even though I was constantly exhausted with M.E, it was very hard to drop off to sleep, and surely if I had nodded, I would have been aware of it. Your head bobs, and it wakes you up. I am also a massive drooler. When I do have a nap outside of bedtime, if I have been so exhausted that I put myself to bed, I always wake up in a pool of drool. Why is that? Not a bit at regular bedtime but I resemble Homer Simpson if I have a nap. I had definitely not been drooling. I had most certainly lost more than twenty Earth minutes.

Then a real calmness came over me, and I began fully to understand once again what had happened. I didn't hear voices, but it was as if somebody had given me the information. I suddenly had the knowledge that I had taken this small boy back to the other side and told him to wait for me there. I don't know where it came from, but a lot of information has come to me over the years in this way, as if it is impressed into my consciousness or I am in tune with the telepathic nature of spirit, so don't need to hear a voice. I just know certain things. This doesn't happen all the time for sure, and I have no control over it, but it seems that when I am supposed to know something, or they want me to know something, the information is instantly there, available in my head, as it was that night with the funny Medusa head. I questioned it quite a lot and figured I was going crazy. Well you would, wouldn't you? You would question your sanity. I am a chronic over-thinker, and it bamboozled me. Once I learned just to accept it, it made life much easier.

Life carried on, and all was quiet for a little while. The M.E was its usual completely and utterly draining self. Sleep did not do anything to alleviate the constant exhaustion, but I learned to pace myself and use my energy like a bank account. Every day I had a pound to spend while others had four or five. My pound had to be spent wisely, and some things were more expensive than others, with emotions the most expensive of all. Just living a very basic day took all of that money and more. I could borrow a little from an overdraft (pushing beyond my limits), but that came with heavy interest. If I pushed a few hours, it didn't take the same amount of rest to recover a few hours could take a few weeks to recover. In fact, the next day could sometimes feel like I had gotten away with it. It is a deadly thing, this M.E. It can lull you into a false sense of security. It would be twenty-four to forty-eight hours after pushing myself that I would hit the brick wall and be confined to my bed once more.

In those days, though, it was a little more flexible than it is now. Twenty years on and, year on year, it has become worse. The ability to borrow has become less and at some points has stopped completely. I have been literally on my knees on the floor crying that I just can't take anymore. The head pain from the almost constant migraines has more than once made me contemplate getting my chainsaw out, or my big axe. However, being the absolute klutz that I am, I probably would have made an error and not end up dead but injured, and my life would be even worse than before. Jacob has sat with me on that floor, holding me and comforting me, not knowing what to do. Bless him – it's a good job he is a strong kid.

Matt and I found out that I was pregnant again, it was a surprise, but we loved Jacob so much, and Matt would have very much been in his element with a little girl, so we were happy. Scared but happy. Within a couple of weeks, however, I started to get very sick. I was bedridden and unable to look after Jacob properly. Matt was taking time off that he couldn't afford. Over the next few weeks, things just got worse and worse. It got to the point where we both realised that we couldn't carry on.

My body was no longer well enough to carry a baby safely, either for the baby or me. We had to make the choice that the wellbeing of Jacob and myself came first. It was the hardest decision, and it broke both our hearts, as we loved being parents.

The day came to go to the clinic, and I felt numb. I remember taking a tablet and then sitting waiting for it to happen. It was soul-destroying. I had to keep going to the bathroom and passing what came out into a bowl, giving that to the nurse to check the contents. I saw, briefly, a small little yellow-coloured waxy-looking bean like a canned butter bean. Tears streaming down my face, I knew what I had seen. I quickly gave the bowl to the nurse. She came back and said the worst was over and I had passed what I needed to. I went home and took to my bed for some days. My body was still feeling very ill, but my soul was even sicker. The guilt still lives with me, and I still wonder what that child would have been like.

I feel bad for Ja being an only child. As a kid, he wanted siblings. He relished the idea of having a brother or sister. I know now, seeing what a fine young man he is, what a fabulous older brother he would have made. As it was, it meant we were even more dedicated to Ja and felt even luckier that we did get this one chance. Now, Ja would tell you he is happy being the only child and not sharing anything, including his mum and dad.

Whilst this was all happening, and I was feeling poorly and very low, we had a visit from Matt's dad, Salvatore. In the beginning, when I first met Matt, Salvatore struck me as being very charming, the suavity that comes from the huge egos the Italian men I have met seem to have. "Everything that is Italian is the best in the world. Italy is the best country in the world," they said. There is a sense that there is an 'I am better than you because I am Italian,' thing going on there. Behind those smouldering brown eyes that my mum loved (mind, as I said before, she had a way of liking the wrong men), I could see a much crueller, troubled man, a man who never filled the potential he thought he had, a man who figured life had been unkind to him. Something about him never sat right with me. The hairs on the back of my neck would stand up if he got too close to me.

He turned out to be your typical old school chauvinist, worked in a factory but thought he was a don. In marriage, he thought he had a right to look for sex elsewhere if his wife didn't give him any. For these reasons, Matt's mum split with him. He had an affair with a woman in the pizza restaurant where he worked, and spent all their money going to the casino until the small hours. Here was a man who demanded Liliana get his medication for him, barked orders for her to cut his fingernails and toenails and run around after him treating him like a baby. Never once did I hear him ask nicely or say thank you to her. However, he had paid for our hotel on the first visit to Italy. He had included me like one of the family and introduced me to the whole lot of them.

There were four brothers, Matt's dad being the eldest. Mario was rocking the 'super Mario from Nintendo' look, with his handlebar moustache and jolly personality. He was a builder and had done reasonably well for himself. Filippo was a middle brother too. He was Father Christmas without a doubt, complete with snowy white beard, a soft, quiet and kind persona, and he owned a toyshop in Rome, so he really was Santa! Tonino was the baby, built the same as the other three, with a shiny, bald pate and a pot belly. He was the cutest of them, although he was nicknamed Godzilla for his eating capacity. He had also done well owning a petrol station and a garage by the coast. So adding to Salvatore's 'woe' was the fact he was the least successful of them. Liliana, his wife, didn't speak any English, and we didn't speak Italian so he was always the translator, until a few years later when I could understand a reasonable amount and get by with my pigeon Italian.

He came to visit while I had been poorly, without Liliana. She was not great at leaving Italy in the beginning. Without her there and whilst Matt was at work, he started to show his true colours. I remember clearly, that when I was sitting in my pyjamas feeling very unwell but trying to be sociable and not stay in bed, he said to me, "I don't think you know how lucky you are."

"Sorry?" I said.

"Look what my son has provided for you. I have a string of girls back home in Italy who would give their right arm to be in your position." Therefore, any time I stepped out of line, there was a ready supply chain.

I was too weak to argue. He had clearly forgotten that I was my own woman before I met Matt, with my own home and not a penny of debt. Matt had his place too but had a couple of grand on credit cards from buying gadgets, his favourite thing. He also made it clear that I was too outspoken and that my place was in the kitchen and rearing babies. My God, this man was straight out of a cave. I know he had a furrowed brow as Matt does, but you could trace this guy straight back to the Neanderthals. They were not extinct, they had just moved to Italy!

Later in the week, to top it off, Matt was ironing his work uniform. I have never thought of ironing as one of my strong points. The clothes go under the iron and somehow come out with extra wrinkles ironed in. I think it is because I am little and don't have the power to press hard, so Matt would often do this task. That night once again, he came to me on the attack. "How do you think it makes me feel to see my son doing a woman's job like ironing?" Hang on, I was not going to let him railroad me again. I was not some domineering housewife who made her husband do menial tasks.

"Ermm, well, actually you should feel proud. Firstly, he ironed his own clothes long before I came along, and secondly, it was the Marines who taught him to iron, and you can't get more manly than that, can you?"

He fell silent. I may have been feeling poorly, but as Matt would tell me years later, I would be wagging my finger on my deathbed. Nobody gets the better of me for too long! I take it and take it for the sake of keeping the peace. Then I can let rip. I was calm though, that night and for the many years I saw him after that. He was Jacob's Grandad, and if nothing else, he loved Ja and Ja loved him back. Poor Matt often got the backlash, though, when time had been spent with the in-laws. He was stuck between a rock and a hard place. Thank goodness he went home and never followed through with his plan to come and live in England. I think you would have found me either in a lunatic asylum or in jail doing life.

Once he was gone, things settled down again, I was still very poorly, and after having no spooky goings-on for a few weeks, I was awoken by Jacob in the night. It was one single very strange noise, not even a cry. I woke quickly and opened my eyes to see that there at the bottom of the bed on my side were two figures. There was a male and a female, and they were looking at me. I was stunned for a few seconds. They were not burglars as they were not 3D solid, but they were as 3D as a solid body. How can I describe it to you? At the time, on TV there was an advert for Evian water, I think. It was two people running, but they were made from water. It was a bit like that. They were almost see-through, but so detailed that they looked completely solid, and sparkling as if the brightest light was shining on them like human-shaped, multifaceted diamonds shimmering in the sun. The lady had a bob haircut. I remember it well. She was little, smaller than the male, maybe around five feet tall. The male was maybe my height, around five feet, five inches.

I was not freaked out. In fact, I was very peaceful, but it was such an unusual thing to happen that I didn't want to acknowledge what I was seeing. My heart felt a beautiful warmth and serenity, but my head was asking what the hell was happening. I put the covers over my head and in no uncertain terms told them to go away! There was no explanation for what I had seen, so it just could not register in my scientific brain. I looked again from under the covers, and they were gone. I questioned my sanity and dropped back off to sleep.

When I woke the next morning, I asked Matt if he had heard Ja. He said he had not. I told him what I had seen, and he took it as normally as if I told him I had seen a fly; as if it was nothing out of the ordinary. I guess he probably thought I was bonkers or hallucinating, but was being kind. I soon forgot about it and went about my day.

That night we went to bed again as normal. I was awoken again by that very same strange cry from Jacob. I opened my eyes, and right there again was the female at the end of the bed. I wasn't going to tell her to go away again, as that clearly didn't work for long. This time I was much more intrigued. It couldn't be two nights hallucinating a similar thing surely? It felt very real too, the most real thing I had ever experienced. That is hard to understand I'm sure, but it was the most vivid thing, as if everything else in life was seventy-five per cent and she was a hundred per cent.

She started to move towards me, so I figured I would just watch her. She rose up and moved parallel above me. It all seemed very calm, and I had no fear whatsoever. I just hoped she would not come too close, as I didn't know what spirits were capable of. As I looked at her, she lined herself up above me. I could see the fine features of her petite face looking down at me (my life was getting weirder by the day). I started to look away from her face down to her shoulders. It was then I saw the outline of something around her at the sides. It was feathery wings. OMG She was an angel! Angels were real, and there was one in my bedroom directly above me! She had come back to show me not to be afraid.

I just carried on watching as she moved upwards further and further until she had dissipated up by the ceiling. What had I just seen? OK, am I awake? Who on earth would ever believe me? Can I or should I tell people? I had an urge to jump out of bed and knock on people's doors like some mad celestial messenger. Hang on; this could still be a dream surely? Maybe I am still asleep? But then, I am lying here, having what seems to be a weird but reasonable conversation with myself (something I found I am quite good at). So I grabbed a scrap of paper off my bedside table and scribbled 'I am awake' and moved my wedding rings off my finger and put them on the table. I then booted Matt in the side and asked him if I was awake. He said, "Yes, and now I am!" Oops. I somehow managed through all the crazy thoughts to drop back off to sleep.

The next morning Matt recalled me waking him, and the rings and paper were there beside me. I told Matt again what had happened, and he once again took it as if it was an everyday occurrence, which of course it had been the last two nights. He was so calm about it, almost as if he was already in the know, which of course he wasn't. Still, I think there had been enough strange things happening the last few months to make him think that anything was possible. As long as he didn't have to see it himself, he was happy for me to tell him my stories. I think it connected him to me and to the Universe in a way he wouldn't even have begun to understand physically. Looking back, I can see that he took peace and comfort from my experiences.

The next night I went off to sleep not knowing if I would be presented with celestial beings again, but trying not to think too much about it. I slept right through, as did Jacob. If we had visitors, neither of us were aware of it. Phew, I don't think I could have handled three in a row.

Matt went off to work his nightshift the following evening, and I went in to check on Ja on my way to bed. As usual, I left his door ajar, and mine too. This allowed me to see across the hallway to his room. That was my little routine when Matt was out. I was always a bit nervous when he was on nights. I would be wary of strange noises and sometimes dreamt of burglars coming up the stairs. I wouldn't be able to scream, I was so afraid. I think that is why I eventually moved to the middle of nowhere. Anyway, that night I eventually dropped off to sleep. Once again, in the middle of the night, I heard the now-familiar single cry. As I woke, I was once again looking straight at this little female with a blunt bob. It was as if my soul knew where she was. I was already seeing her and my eyes were exactly on her even though she wasn't in my room. She was peeping round the doorway, looking at me as if to say, "Oh no, I woke him again." Then she moved upwards and dissipated into thin air once more.

I checked on Ja, but he had not moved. He had been totally unaware that he was warning me of my visitor. His soul must have been aware of who was around us. After that night, I didn't see the little angel again for a long time, but she left me with a legacy because, from that point onwards, the Universe opened up to me.

So much happened over the coming months and years that it is very hard to know where to start and stop. How much to write about all that has happened over the last sixteen years, and how crazy it all sounds, is worth another book in its own right, I guess. I had started to jot down all of my experiences, usually right after they happened, so it was in very scrawling handwriting in my type of shorthand notes.

The unusual things I saw, I usually tried but failed to give a very rough drawing. I was never any good at art, although I am quite creative and enjoy card making and jewellery making. I draw like a five-year-old. Thankfully, when I read that little notebook, I can still see every image clearly, from the original Angels to…Aliens. I think the FBI would have a field day probing my brain.

Well, I guess more my soul - I am not sure it is my brain.

Why me? What did they want? Did they visit everyone but only I saw them? Did they know me, my soul? I have no idea. I have spoken to many mediums and spiritually connected people, most of whom have contact in some way to our deceased loved ones. But, nobody I have talked to has had multiple visits from astral beings too. They say that approximately five per cent of humans see spirit and five per cent of those see spirit with their open eyes rather than their mind's eye. Now, seventeen or so years on, I too 'feel' this connection more often than seeing them with open eyes as before.

However, there are no statistics for those people who see, or, as in my case, get visits from, beings from other worlds. Yes, I know it sounds completely bizarre. Believe me, when it first started happening to me, it was the weirdest thing, and I have been very careful who I have told, as sometimes it hasn't been received that well. I am not crazy, not in the mental health way anyway, although always quirky and slightly cookie I have been told — and Jacob calls me goofy — but completely and utterly sane. I am the first to debunk weird stuff.

By this point I had seen a good many humans, most of whom I did not recognise. Some were next to me, others on Matt's side of the bed. I saw animals too and started to see people's totem animals, the animal representation of yourself. I saw mine a few times. It alternated between a lion and a tiger. However, the tiger is my animal. She is a white Siberian tiger, and she often walks with my Native American spirit guide, Skylark.

I felt him long before I ever saw him, and have only seen him a couple of times. A strong and solemn-looking, craggy-faced man, but beautiful and kind. He is my protector and was in a native Indian life that we shared. Even as I write, he is making it known that he feels uncomfortable being described in writing. 'Craggy' was not his choice of word. 'Etched by life and wise' are how he would describe himself. He appears to be wearing long dark hair, as you would expect, and wears neutral-coloured (I assume some kind of hide) basic-shaped, practical clothes. He offers very little in the form of help, and he is solely there to protect me from harm. He cannot and will not — he emphasised the WILL NOT there — help influence any decision I make.

You see, we come here to make those decisions based on our own free will. That is the greatest gift the Universe gives us. We also learn all of our lessons based on those decisions of our own free will. To interfere would be to take that free will from us. Therefore, as much as we all like a little guidance (and many people seek help from mediums to see what the future holds), it is not written in stone. Long before we come into a body, we sit with our soul group and write the lessons we wish to learn this time around. Our soul group intertwines their lessons with ours, and we set our milestones. These milestones we will come to at some point on our journey. How we get to those and what we do with those lessons when we get there is our own free will.

I guess it is like walking down the road of life. Every side road will eventually come out at that same place. We can choose side road after side road and walk for many, many more miles (not necessarily pleasant) than we need to, and we do. However, we cannot miss the lesson. That is not to say we will learn from it, and we put before ourselves many of the same lessons repeatedly. Some are about certain people, and the lesson is to keep away from them, but it is very hard to pull away from the draw of the familiar. I think this is one of the most difficult lessons because it is of the heart. I am sure many of you reading this have known you should stay away from someone, but the rose-tinted glass of the rear-view mirror distorts and softens what we have experienced. Our compassion and tendency to remember the good things allow us to be drawn back into that lesson all over again. It is not necessarily just a love relationship either. My own flawed father and my drug-addled brother have sucked me back countless times. I am amongst the biggest suckers for this lesson. Try to remember that sometimes we too have agreed to sacrifice our own heart and be hurt ourselves to help someone else in their spiritual soul growth.

I have always been a dreamer, always trying to push forward and keep life changing. I crave change. However, in some ways, I seek to change everything else around me, perhaps because there is one fundamental part of myself I can't change, which is my health. I think it is also because I had so much change in my childhood -- except for those few stable Cayton years, things were always uncertain and unstable. I have had a transient lifestyle throughout my adult years too, that is, until I bought my house and met Matt. I crave stability and security on the one hand but run from it on the other. I guess we are all a product of our upbringing, with the ups and downs that happen in childhood and adolescence, how our parents bring us up, the things they tell us, the love and support they offer us, or don't.

Since I was a little girl, I always thought that I wanted to be a gypsy traveller, exploring the world with my home right behind me. Maybe the explorer in me and my need for stability and security were rolled into one right there in that dream. I didn't over-analyse everything as a girl like I do now, although I did find out from my dad's family that we have Roma gypsy heritage, so that makes sense too -- it's in my blood.

Poor Matt! Being with me, he got the whole force of my spontaneous, whimsical dithering. At one point, I had him seriously thinking about moving to Australia to join the police WAPOL and SAPOL, and the same for Canada with the Canadian police force. He did take these options seriously, as they would have been jobs he knew well. Anyway, this didn't work out, as my mum had been diagnosed with Crohn's disease, and it was just too far to go and leave her. It had taken doctors two years to diagnose her as they just told her she had IBS even though she had a very clear family history of Crohn's. Meanwhile, she lost half her body weight and dropped down to five stones, although she wore layers of baggy clothes to disguise this from us. There was no way she could fly such a long distance, either.

I also had Matt thinking about opening an estate agent in mainland Spain, or an ice cream stand in Majorca. His feet were firmly stuck in the soil here in the end, but he allowed me to dream and come up with ideas because he knew how important that was to me. I was stuck inside this body, which no longer worked properly. I felt trapped inside, so overwhelmingly exhausted and unable to work. I couldn't commit to anyone a date or time as my brain was constantly in a thick, clouded fog. These dreams helped me remove myself from the limitations that M.E put on me. I could sit, for however long my brain or eyes would work for, and search new lands and opportunities. Then I could close my eyes if I was confined to my bed, and go off into a place in my mind where I could play out these new dreams. I didn't have to be the 'me with M.E'. In my mind, I was the old me, full of life and energy.

Chapter Ten

In the end, I had put so much thought and
energy in wanting to be abroad that Matt finally
agreed we could take out some extra mortgage
(our house value had gone up quite a bit) and
buy a cheapie property abroad. I had already
looked at property in just about every country in
the world. (God knows what I would have done
in those days before the internet. It was my
saviour) I had already looked seriously at Spain,
Portugal, Morocco, the Greek islands, the
Canaries (our favourite holiday destination) and
Bulgaria (which was super cheap for a 'do it up
yourself' place). Then I found a website
dedicated to ex-pats buying in Turkey, especially
along the Aegean coast around the Kusadasi to
Bodrum area.

We had never been to Turkey before, but I
had lived in Saudi, and holidayed in Tunisia and
Greece so had a vague idea. I scoured the
website from top to bottom and read everything
I could. According to Terry and John, who ran
the website, they had moved across from the
UK two years before and were doing great. I
saw properties in their village that looked
interesting but one day came across a 'for sale'
post somewhere else. I fell in love with the
place immediately, and Matt liked it, which
was a good response, as he rarely got excited. I
knew there, and then that was my house, or

one the same as that. We decided that we would go to see the property in the winter, because if we liked it then, we would love it in the summer.

With the help of Terry and John (who recommended a hotel and their estate agent who they trusted completely), Matt, Jacob and I set off for Turkey in January 2005 on a wonderful adventure. We flew in via Istanbul and down to Izmir, our estate agent picking us up at the airport and taking us to our hotel. Wow! The welcome we got was amazing.

Turkey seemed gritty but real, not polished like Florida by any means and not as Arabic and strict as Saudi Arabia. To me, it felt like a wonderful mix of the feeling of the Mediterranean with the background of familiarity and nostalgia that the call to prayers and the mosques brought me. Jacob took everything in his stride as he always did.

The first day we were greeted bright and early by John. He took us to see some properties in his home village of Guzelçamli, nestled at the edge of the national park. It was beautiful. It had once just been a small fishing village but had grown quite a lot. The properties we went to see needed finishing, but you could get an idea of how they would be. For me though, I wanted to be somewhere else as this area didn't feel quite right. John took us off to meet Terry and their daughter

Neala, for lunch at a local restaurant, the Agora. I can't remember what we ate, except I remember Jacob had big beans.

Terry and John were just the best people you could wish to meet. We immediately hit it off and became good friends, always visiting them whenever we were back in Turkey. The second day, our estate agents Ali and Hussein, came to pick us up, laden with fresh spinach and white cheese borek made by his neighbour for our breakfast. 'Ben', the owner, had put more delights out for us too. Sometimes, when you do things in life, they feel awkward and unsettling when they are new. This felt like every road had led here, as if we were meant to be here, right now, and there was never anywhere else we could be.

We went off looking at properties that they had chosen for us, given our requirements. A few of them were in the ladies' beach area and nearby on the flat part towards Davultar, near the long beaches. Matt very much liked one of them, but once again, that feeling was there. None of them was what I was looking for, as they were all too squashed together. I just had a bee in my bonnet. I showed Ali the picture of the house that I had held onto for dear life. 'Can you take us here?' I asked. "Oh," he replied, "We looked at that site but deemed it not suitable, as it's a hard walk with a buggy."

Nevertheless, off we went. Hussein started driving up a long and winding, hilly road and I could see a site off in the distance on the right. I knew that was the one. As we drove through the tiny dusty village, I could see just local people, a couple of mini-market shops, a seasonal butcher and the obligatory chai room for the men. We turned off the main road and headed down a bumpy rubble track for a good half mile. The road starting going steeply downhill and there we were, Dagçilar Sitesi. Built on a very steep slope some fifteen years before, were a hundred identical semi-detached villas, some all nice and polished, others not quite finished.

In Turkey, you buy the plot, and then when you save up some more, you put foundations in, etc. The site was initially for people who lived in Izmir and Istanbul to have a summerhouse in the mountains. The streets were lined with mature trees such as orange, plum and pomegranate. As you looked down the street, you could see the national park and Guzelçamli in the distance and the bay of the Aegean. Off to the right side, opposite the national park, you could see the Greek island of Samos on a clear day. This was it. I had to live here. There was nowhere else. The 'me who didn't have ME' did not care one jot about the hill, the half-mile rubble and the dust road. All I saw was home, peace and serenity.

Matt was equally captivated.

There were also plans in the pipeline for a shared pool to be built, which made it seem even more perfect. Ali found the site handyman, Ekrem, and asked him if there were any for sale. He said there were one or two and took us off to see one at the bottom of the hill. It was beautiful, just like the picture, and from the roof terrace, you could see the bay. We asked the price and agreed to have it. However, it turned out the owner did not want to sell at that price to foreigners. That was the Turkish price.

We found this to be quite a common thing in Turkey. There was the Turkish price and the foreigner price. It was always best to buy from the market where there were price labels. Many people were fair, and if you bartered and asked for the Turkish price, they would laugh. On the other hand, someone would say, "They live here, they aren't tourists. Give them a good price." The handyman made some calls, and the next day we went to see one on the front line. It was beautiful but at a ridiculous price and had just been finished. It was near the top of the site, so less hill to climb. The ground floor was below street level, meaning it would stay cool in the summer. As we entered, it was like walking into your own home. It was mine. I knew it.

A small kitchen lay to the left and an open plan living room diner to the right, along with a downstairs bathroom. A big wraparound covered terrace to the front, and a small roofed terrace off the kitchen, with gorgeous mountain views. Up the marble staircase were two good-sized bedrooms, each with balconies, with the front another wrap round and the back a small one with mountain views again. Another bathroom sandwiched in between the bedrooms. Then another marble staircase leading to the upper floor where you found another good-sized bedroom, a laundry room and the most fabulous feature of the house, a big roof terrace with a built-in BBQ. The hilly road afforded the roof terrace the most beautiful view of the national park and the Aegean and Samos. Although it was not straight ahead but to the left, it did not matter. This was my house. I just felt it.

The house was up for an absolute steal. The man who owned it had ran out of money. Ali and Hussein were amazing, quickly making it clear they didn't trust the seller's motives. They came back to us with an amazing proposition. They would buy the house for us with their cash. House transactions are done in a day in Turkey. If there are any debts on the house, they go to the next buyer, and they did not want us to fall into a trap in a country where we did not even understand the language. Terry and John assured us they trusted Ali and Hussein one hundred per cent, so we went with their offer. Within a day, the house was bought.

In the space of a week, we had gone off to Turkey, a country we had never even visited before, and bought a house. It did not seem like a big deal to us, but it did to our family and friends when we told them.

The last night we were there, we treated ourselves to a meal out. We had been recommended a kebab place in Kusadasi called "Bulbul". It was very popular local establishment. One of the waiters welcomed us in and explained the menu to us. We ordered by pictures. Starting with something that looked like pizza called pide (with eggs and cheese), followed by kebab. I had a stew called guvec, I think, then finished with rice pudding, called sutlac, all gobbled down with glass bottles of coca-cola. The bill came to less than £10. We were hooked. Jacob was greeted by everyone with the friendliest of welcomes. Being blond and blue-eyed and small, he was a lucky charm for the locals.

While walking down the street one day while we were out exploring, we saw two burly guys with typical huge moustaches. As they walked past they started talking loudly, swept Jacob off his feet and started swinging him around, landing huge prickly kisses all over him! The Turkish people love children, but Jacob's blue eyes were like the lucky Turkish eye charm, boncuk, which wards away evil spirits. It was an incredible adventure, and it had only just begun.

We had maxed ourselves out so much we had to sell our little caravan to be able to afford to furnish the house, but it was worth it. The first time we visited our own home, we furnished it with what we could get, which at the time was very springy L shaped sofas that folded down to make the most uncomfortable bed, which made it feel as if you were trying to sleep on a two-humped camel. We did find fabulous beds, though, ones that lifted up ottoman style, where we could store lots of things. Basic wardrobes, some other bits and pieces, and we were set. I think we bought everything in one day and it was all delivered that day or the next. If you were buying stuff, delivery was usually fantastic. If you needed a workman to do something, they all worked on Turkish time, which had no relevance to the time they told you, sometimes not even the day. At first, Matt, used to the English way of things, got a bit wound up. Once he realised it wasn't personal, he learned to take it as it came.

On our first holiday there, the plum tree right outside our house was teeming with tiny little unripe purple plums. I watched from my window as many people would stop and pick a few. I couldn't understand this, as they were only the size of grapes. I had a go, in case I was missing out on a treat, but they were so sour and astringent. I learned from Terry that they are eaten like that and often dipped in salt. Peaches, apricots and plums were all eaten way before they were ripe, but I guess when times are hard, and you are hungry you can't afford to wait for the crop to ripen. It was a taste gained from days of poverty, I suppose. By year two or three, I would pick them occasionally and have a nibble myself. The sourness almost had an addictive quality to it.

Our neighbour at the back of the house was Ekrem, the handyman. He lived there with his wife Yasmin and their son, Gurkam, who was just a few months older than Jacob. Gurkam loved coming round to play with Ja. Even though they didn't speak the same language, they both knew the international language of play. Gurkam would come knocking on the door all the time. He would head straight for the fridge as it would be full of things they could not afford on a handyman's salary. He sometimes stayed for tea. It was fun for them both.

As they got older, they were allowed down to the park on their own to play. Gurkam would climb trees and pick fruit for them to eat. He showed us how to eat a pomegranate freshly picked from a tree. Just stick your teeth in and bite the yellow skin and pith away. Picked fresh, they were softer and easier to unravel than how we were used to them at home, where the skin had become dry and shrank tightly to the fruit. It was very much a learning curve, too, as many things were different.

I tried to make a cake one day, as I loved all the fabulous ingredients available at the market. My little Turkish scales had not been designed well, and with food being weighed in the bowl, would often become unstable. I only found this out when a bowl full of sugar went everywhere, including under the kitchen bench. I cleaned it up as best as I could and thought no more of it as we went out on the local bus into town. I arrived home to so many tiny ants that I believe every ant in Turkey was in my kitchen. They had marched inside in their neat line formation and taken over every surface, inside and out of the cupboards. I nearly freaked out. Well I probably did freak out. The next couple of hours were spent cleaning up that army of little ants, looking meticulously inside every packet and box.

From that day onwards everything was in sealed jars, clipped shut, tightly packed. Bleach went under my units to kill the smell of sugar. Every mealtime was a session of paranoia. Every tiny crumb was watched and carefully cleared away. Dinner was taken on the roof terrace as it was so much easier to clean up there, and the ants didn't bother if there were crumbs. Occasionally we made mistakes, like forgetting to throw an onion or potato out before we left for home, but, for the most part, we learned quickly as to what worked and didn't.

Sometimes if I felt I had the energy, I would go out a week or two before Matt to get everything ready for him when he arrived. It was an exciting time for Jacob and me. He was still only little, maybe around three or four years old. On the first day would be our supermarket shop and the next, the fruit and vegetable market, or vice versa depending which day we arrived. We would go out for lunch and come back with our wheelie trolley stocked with essentials.

Near the Friday fruit and vegetable market was the dolmus station. These were the little buses that went all over the place and would pick you up or drop you off anywhere along their route. I was beginning to be recognised a little, as we got on and off the dolmus from our village quite often. The dolmus station manager would recognise me too, and when he saw me, would cross the busy road to get my bags and put me on the right bus. The dolmus drivers were good too. One in particular, whose name I never knew, but had the loveliest friendly face and the obligatory moustache, would take me down the rubble track out of his way, so I had less of a journey with my shopping.

They were all protective of Ja and me. I felt completely safe when we were there alone. I was never once hit upon (although I never went down the touristy streets where this was more common). They had a respect for me because I was a mummy, I think. Most of the days, though, we spent at home resting so that when I needed to get stuff, I could go out. M.E was still the hardest thing to deal with, but the sunshine really did help.

One morning I was lying in bed when Jacob came wandering through, talking to me. I was still very, very tired as it had been market day the day before, so I was still in bed. He started to wander back through to his own bedroom, walking past the opening of the winding marble staircase. Then he turned back round to talk to me and as he did so, slipping on the tiles and stepping backwards. Life suddenly went in slow motion. I saw him falling backwards down the marble stairs. In a split second, his little arms came out and grabbed onto the handrail at one side and the decorative metal support at the other, so he was able to pull himself upright. All I could do was watch in amazement, as even though I had jumped out of bed, it was all over in the shortest time but the longest time. That doesn't make sense I know, but time did not go as normal in what seemed like those few seconds. How did a three/four-year-old save himself from what would have been a deadly injury? His arms could barely even stretch from one side of the stairs to the other. It was an unfamiliar setting too. In those minutes after it happened, once my heart started beating again, I realised that Jacob had been saved; that someone had been behind him and held him long enough for him to be able to grab the rails. That day he was saved, I believe, by the angels. It was one of his nine lives.

After visiting a few times in the first year, we decided longer stays were better, with less travelling and feeling more settled. Mum would look after our Westie dogs, Dolly and Katie, and stay in our house. This gave her a break from her own little flat. She didn't have to worry about electric, heating or food, and I always made sure the fridge was stocked. I would ring periodically from the payphone in the village, once I worked out how to use it. We had been gone three weeks on one of these early trips when I rang Mum to confirm what time we would be home. She seemed in good spirits and said all was well, and the dogs had been fine. We were getting in at 'silly' o'clock, so she shouldn't wait up, and we would see her in the morning.

All was normal on the trip home. We arrived into Newcastle around two or three a.m., got to the house, greeted the dogs and went straight to bed. Jacob of course decided that he would like to get up early with the birds as usual. Therefore, Matt got up with him while I had a bit extra rest. I got up mid-morning and decided to make my famous bolognese, so that my mum could take some home with her.

Busy in the kitchen I didn't notice time

was ticking by. It got to lunchtime and Mum still had not risen, so I knocked on the door and asked if she was getting up, as lunch was ready. I didn't get a reply, so I went back downstairs and tried again half hour later. Mum had chronic insomnia and had taken temazepam for thirty-odd years. She barely slept at night and often slept in the morning instead, so it wasn't unusual for her to be sleeping late. I knocked once more on the door with no answer. I told her to get up and get ready and walked off.

Shortly after, I heard shuffling, and she brought herself down the stairs. She walked, well bounced, off the walls into the kitchen barely able to move her feet. I could see by her eyes and demeanour that something was seriously wrong. I just had a feeling what it was. I put a chair outside, sat her on it to get some fresh air, and ran upstairs to see if the bedroom held any clues. There on the floor were empty bottles, packets and pills. In her completely zoned out mind, she had not even thought of the ramifications had Jacob gone upstairs before me and seen Nana had left 'sweets' on the floor.

I ran downstairs and started shouting at her, "What have you done? How many have you taken?" I was frantic. She denied everything, but she was clearly in another world. I told her I knew what she had done and that I was not only extremely mad at her for doing it, but that she did it in my home. What if she had succeeded?

She had taken enough meds to kill an elephant. What if Jacob had found her? Matt reminded me she was not in a fit state for one of my well-known lectures. I had no choice but to call an ambulance. I didn't know when she had taken them. The effects could still get much worse.

It didn't take long for the ambulance to come, and I went with her to the hospital. The doctor quickly came round to assess her, and I told her what had happened. She helped Mum take her top off for examination. I nearly fell through the floor with shock. There before me was a shell of my mum. She was skeletal, just bones and skin and nothing else. Her once B Cup boobs were reduced to two uninflated party balloons. She looked on the verge of death. I guess it just hadn't shown in her face because we girls in the family have quite bony faces anyway.

She had been suffering with her tummy. I knew she had a lot of pain, but the doctor told her she had IBS. This was later to be diagnosed correctly as Crohn's disease, something that ran in our family. I had been very busy having M.E, having a baby and trying to bring him up. I hadn't visited her as much as I could have, but I didn't drive at that time. I relied upon Matt, and he was already spending his off time running us around as we needed.

The doctor asked her a series of questions, all which she answered as if it was fifty years ago. Even King George was still the monarch. It turns out the meds had all been absorbed, and she just hadn't taken enough. It was enough for any normal person, but she had a high tolerance to temazepam after thirty-plus years of increasing doses.

She said later that the pain had gotten too much for her to take and she hadn't wanted to deal with it anymore. She didn't want to leave the dogs on their own, so figured the night we came back was her night. She had planned it. It wasn't spontaneous. That is why she sounded so happy and jolly on the phone as she had thought her ordeal was soon to be over. It took some time for all the side effects to wear off, but that was Mum's lowest point. She could only go upwards from there. Ricky had been working back home in Scarborough, and he came back to move in and take care of her. I am not sure if it was due to him taking care of her, or just being there, but it helped her refocus. She had company, and that was important. It took me a long time to forgive her for what she did. At the same time, I understand it had been the act of a desperate woman, who had had enough of the unrelenting pain. My house forever felt tainted. I could not go in the room she had used. I changed the furniture, but the darkness stayed in the air.

Chapter Eleven

I didn't realise at the time how sensitive I was
becoming to everything around me. It was as if
all of my senses were developing. My hearing
was getting sharper, and I could hear everything
more clearly. Visually I was noticing things that I
probably wouldn't have noticed before. I could
taste and identify many ingredients in foods. I
started to gain insight into things, and I didn't
know where that was coming from. I guess I just
put it down to strong instinct. The amount of
visitors I had seemed to be increasing too. I had
seen my own guides and the Angels, as well as
some other random people and floating eyes or
noses (these latter either didn't have the energy
to fully manifest or I was tired at the time and
couldn't tune in properly).

I woke one night to see a black panther
standing up on its hind legs and looking out of
my window. I lay looking at it for about thirty
seconds before it must have realised I was
awake. It turned its head towards me, looked
and saw I was nothing of interest, and then
turned its head back to the window. It was such
a regal-looking animal. I was in awe of its
majesty. I knew it was Matt's totem animal. I just
started acknowledging the feelings I was getting
that did not come from me. I knew that I was
tuning into a radio station that had all the
information. It was no surprise though that Matt

had a panther (I always joked he must be a silverback gorilla as that is what Matt reminded me of) as it was poised and dignified and a bit of a loner. It was a big cat, a big softy, but it would attack you if cornered. It is one of those animals you can't quite figure out, Tigers and lions we see a lot and know their persona, but a panther is rarer and more elusive. I sometimes saw other animals too, such as little dogs or horses, depending where I was.

Then one night, the weirdest thing happened. I was asleep with Matt when a noise awoke me. As I opened my eyes, I was looking directly to the corner of my room. My wardrobes were along one wall and round the corner a bit. Right on this corner, I could see three beings. They most definitely were not human, and were very similar to the typical description of 'Greys' you would see on TV; about four feet tall, light grey in colour with skinny little bodies with two arms and two legs. They had large heads compared to their bodies, with bulbous craniums and tiny facial features, except the eyes, which were black and almond-shaped, but not as big as I had seen on TV. There were two four feet tall ones standing side by side, and one was carrying a smaller one. I would have said it was a baby.

As I was looking at them, absolutely stunned, they were waving at me. All of them, like you would see your neighbours in the street and wave to them. They clearly seemed to recognise me. However, the same couldn't be said for me. I just kept looking and remaining gobsmacked. I was not scared in the slightest. It seemed like a normal thing, because there was no fear whatsoever. I smiled and raised my hand to wave back to them, and as we were waving at each other, they started to dissipate.

I woke Matt to tell him what I had seen and made some quick notes in my notebook. Matt grunted, wondering why I had woken him, and quickly nodded off. Even he wasn't fazed by the fact there had just been astral beings in our bedroom. They too had the appearance of being made from energy just like the others, but I knew the colours. Had they been 3D solid or moving towards me, I think I may have soiled myself! But I took it in my stride, said thank you to the Universe and dozed back off to sleep.

Life was certainly turning out to be surprising, to say the least. In those early days, spirit just seemed to follow me wherever I was; whether at home, visiting friends or family, in Turkey, or even in my caravan. It became so normal to me to see so many and so varied energies. The 'Grey' family certainly were not the last of the astral spirits I have seen. To list them would seem like something George Lucas could have dreamed up. In all of my 'visitations' (I guess you could call them), ninety per cent were silent. Often I saw them mouthing or showing me pictures, but rarely did I get anything. I just apologised and said in my thoughts, "I am sorry, but I cannot hear you." That made me sad and frustrated, and I guess for them too, as I am sure there were some interesting conversations amongst them.

The only definitive information came many years later, around 2013. I had been doing some vigils at Chillingham Castle in Northumberland as a guide, which in itself was an amazing set of experiences and a very interesting story for another day. My spirit radar was turned up to max. I woke up one night in the old converted farm building I lived in to see a red figure. I could see the figure very clearly. I am drawn to say 'she' as the energy felt female. She was humanoid in that she had two arms and two legs. She was covered in red, scaly skin like a snake, with small square scales. There was no hair, just this red colour all over, and eyes the brightest green, much more human-shaped than the typical almond type. They had quite large with a small nose, almost just nostrils, and a small mouth. I lay watching trying to take in all the details of this amazing creature before she dissipated before me.

A couple of weeks went by without incident, and then I was woken by a noise. I opened my eyes and directly in front of me there she was again. This time she was not alone. To the left of her was an identical being, but this one was green. I immediately seemed to be hearing information. I have no idea how this was working, but there seemed to be a connection. I heard that she was female and that all females of the species are red and the males are green. Shocked that I was getting this information, I quickly asked the first thing that came into my mind. "Where are you from?" I asked her through my thoughts, not knowing or believing she would hear me.

"Sumeria," she replied. "It is twenty-five-thousand light-years from here."

I started to see images in my mind's eye. They were of an underground living system -- a large hexagonal domed structure, which was the hub. From it went six domed tunnels to hexagonal-shaped habitational areas. You could not pass from one area to another without going back through the central hub. Whilst you were within this hub, it would scan you and check your health, and you would be updated with all you needed to know. I got the information that the area of Earth that was formally known as Sumeria had been a place that these beings visited, and was named after them. I have not seen those beings since that day, but feel so grateful to have been the recipient of such wonderful information.

As you have read, my experiences with spirit have been quite varied; some would say downright weird, scary or complete fabrication.

I have no wish to tell anything but the absolute truth as I have experienced it. It is bonkers enough without me adding to it! The moment I deviate from the truth is when I put the laptop down and stop writing, because I am writing this initially for my son.

I started my memoirs simply because I knew so very little about my own family. My nan and grandad's earlier lives before I was born remain a mystery to me. They never wanted to talk about how they met or things they got up to, and I only know snippets that my mum told me. Even her life was a mystery. I knew the basic story of the big events, but not in detail, not the things that had made her laugh or shaped her into who she was. So I decided that, given I have had M.E for many years and chronic kidney disease my whole life, I wanted to write all the things down about myself for my son, his kids and their kids. Then if I had an early departure from this mortal world, they would be able to get to know me through my words. In theory, my stories could live forever. Does that sound a bit self-important? I certainly don't think I am any more important than anyone else, but I do think some interesting and varied things have happened, and I want these things to be recorded. Hence, this is the reason you get it as it is without anything added.

Things settled down again after Mum's suicide attempt. We went back to our regular life as much as we could. The M.E was very much up and down, but a constant, unrelenting fatigue was always with me. As long as I was careful and paced myself, I could just about get through everyday basic stuff. I still struggled to make appointments and events or see other people. My life was very much about trying to get through each day. It sometimes got to the point that I let it win and it would take me down to very low places, but I never took meds. Only one time right at the beginning, my GP decided Fluoxetine, also known as Prozac, would possibly give me more energy. All it did was make me want to throw myself from the car at seventy miles an hour on the dual carriageway. It took a lot to control my thoughts that day. I knew I could never take those tablets again. I knew I had to battle this with my own mind. I was strong even if it felt deep down sometimes I was not.

I had started out with the mindset that it was temporary, so as time went on, it seemed more and more hopeless. I decided to look at it differently and see not what it had taken away from me, such as my freedom, choices and cognitive function as well as my bloody energy and occasionally my will to live. I still had my hope, my usual positivity and my beautiful child. I had a loving and supportive husband, a home and food. It had given me time to see a spiritual path I would likely not have otherwise.

It made me appreciate minute things because when you are confined to your bed or home, your perspective on things changes.

For me, the world grew more beautiful, and I took not one bit of it for granted because I was grateful just to wake up and see it. I saw that despite my own personal struggle, things could be much worse. Many people didn't get a chance to wake up today. Every day was a new chance. Hope lived every day. Don't get me wrong. There have still been many times I have been taken down by it, but still I am grateful every day.

The next few years were relatively 'normal' for us. We loved, laughed and cried. We took time to enjoy our amazing boy as he grew. We spent as much time as we could in Turkey. It felt that beyond my illness, all was well. I home-schooled Jacob, as I had a fear of schools given my own experience. This meant I was with him all the time although he did go to a Montessori nursery for socialisation a couple mornings a week. They were fantastic here too, because the manager told me to ring and they would see if they could have him if I was poorly or needed extra rest. He loved going there, but he always played on his own and conversed mostly with the adults and rarely with anyone his own age. He saw them as children, although I don't think he ever saw himself like that. He held quite adult conversations for his age, was wise beyond his years and was smart too. I taught him to read in just a few days while we were in Turkey. He got the concept straight away, and it made total sense to him. Maths, on the other hand, he could not grasp. 1+1 was 11, no matter how many Lego bricks we counted.

Chapter Twelve

It was on one of these little trips Jacob and I would occasionally take to our house when things changed for me. We had been out getting our groceries at the market with our 'old lady' wheelie trolley (fruit and veg was very heavy as you never bought one or two. It was one or two kilos of everything), when suddenly I felt fevered and got a desperate urge for the toilet, OMG, there were no public toilets. I was in the middle of the very busy, crowded Friday market.

I rushed off to the side, trying to think quickly, turning 360° and looking for somewhere to go. A café! Yes, they should have a toilet. I walked in, gave Jacob (who was five at the time) the shopping and told him to sit and wait. I rushed off to the toilet. Time passed by, and I could not leave the cubicle. Every time I thought it was over, it started again. I was dizzy, the pain was unbearable, and I felt like I was going to pass out. Each bout of pain came with the darkness closing in. I couldn't pass out on the toilet. Who would find me? Would it be like Elvis, with me found with my pants around my ankles on the floor?

I tried to pull myself together, but it was no use. I ended up ringing the only people I knew who could come and rescue me, which were Terry and John, who helped find me my house.

Terry lived about thirty kilometres from the town, but she downed tools and came to get me. As I finally got out of the toilet, I saw Jacob and smiled. He had ordered himself some chips and a coke and was happily munching away. I had been gone an hour in the toilet cubicle, but he had barely noticed. The great thing was I knew he would be safe. Turkish people are extremely protective of children. The waiter had kept an eye on him and had seen me rush to the toilet.

Thankfully, Terry took me round to the private hospital, where I was admitted, put on a drip and kept under observation. She took Jacob home to Guzelçamli, where he could be looked after. Terry was amazing. I was so grateful. She came back the next day to pick me up and take me home. Jacob was as black as the ace of spades, with dirt ground under his fingernails, but had had a wonderful time playing with Neala. Terry was also a great cook, so he had been well taken care of.

I was under strict instructions to eat only white foods such as bananas, potatoes, bread or plain yoghurt. I had none in, so thankfully Janice, our neighbour and friend, brought me some bananas. I tried to get myself sorted but still felt awful. Jacob was playing in his bedroom. Suddenly the surge of pain was back, and I was off to the toilet. I sat down and then the blackness came. This time I could not hold on and collapsed off the toilet onto the tiled floor with a thud.

I have no idea how long I was out, but I came round, crawled to my bedroom and got onto my bed. My mobile was on the bedside cabinet, so in tears I called Matt. It feels like a million miles from home when you are alone and sick. Even the comfort of my beautiful home was no match for the safe and secure feeling of being home in the UK with Matt to take care of me. He arranged for our flights home. I stuck everything I could into a heap in my suitcase. Janice and Ian closed up the house. They were brilliant, and because they lived there all year round, they had a key and periodically looked in on our house when we were in the UK.

Once home, it became clear this was not going to be an easy thing to get over. M.E seems to make it much harder to get over viruses or bacterial infections, because your body is already fighting so hard. The only good thing is that I rarely ever get cold or flu. It seems to kick the ass of those! Weeks turned into months, and I was still confined to the house unless Matt took me out. My legs were weak, and if I walked, they felt like they were going to give way. I had half of the little stamina I usually had, and it was not only frustrating but also worrying. I had an MRI for MS, as the symptoms were very similar. Thankfully, that came back clear. This didn't help, though, in finding what was actually going on.

In the end, six months had gone by, and I got to the point where I felt it was time to get a Motability scooter. I contemplated my options, and the only other one was to learn to drive. I had always put this off, as I just didn't think I could master all the gears and instructions. My brain often felt like I was wading through thick mud to find my thoughts. I did not want to panic while out on the roads. Then I found out you could learn to drive in just an automatic car, as people with disabilities do, which would surely be easier. I had a reasonable amount of road sense and knowledge, and it would be far cooler than a Motability scooter.

I set about finding a driving instructor. His name was Bob, and he specialised in automatic lessons for people with disabilities. He was great, if not a little over-friendly. I am quite sure he knew my knee was not the gear stick. However, he got me on the road and gave me confidence. At the same time, I took what little money we saved and bought a little gold-coloured Nissan Micra that I named Betty. Matt could take me out in-between lessons. Even Mum had a driving licence, although she had not been able to afford a car for many years.

I was finally feeling freedom again. Mum started getting the bus down to my house, and we would go out in the car, I had only had one or two lessons by then, but it was irresistible just to get out and drive. We went all over the

Northeast with Jacob in tow. She hadn't a clue where we were going, as she wasn't from this area, so it was nice for her to see new places too. It was quite scary for me, especially when we came to massive roundabouts, as she never helped much with the driving, but I held my nerve and kept going.

I was so proud to be able to get Mum out of the house too. We spent fun days having lunches, and she ate things she couldn't usually eat. She was suffering from narrowing of her oesophagus, likely caused by the Crohn's, and she struggled with potatoes, but managed in that time to eat portions of fish and chips with no ill effects. We also went on picnics (often car picnics) and to local museums.

We finally felt like we were best friends again, and she loved the quality time with Jacob. They completely and utterly adored each other. She fed him ketchup sandwiches and angel cake. They sat together in the same armchair and watched countless episodes of Scooby-Doo or Thomas the Tank Engine when they had alone time together. It was wonderful to see them together. Jacob has always had such a sweetness and chivalry towards women. Goodness knows where he got it from, certainly not from his dad or anyone in my family. He just had and has a way, and still does, of making ladies feel special. We were out and about for around six weeks.

One Friday, Matt had his car in the garage, so he asked if I could pick him up after work. Mum and I had been out, so she wanted a cuppa before we went out again. We got into the house, and she told me that her leg was hurting, Mum's leg always hurt. When she had her varicose vein removed, the surgeon had stitched through or trapped a nerve into the scar. She was always in pain from it, so it wasn't unusual. She took a codeine with a drink of water, but instead of being swallowed, it became stuck in a hole in her tooth, which she was waiting to get filled. I remember it so clearly, because I was rolling with tears of laughter. As the codeine melted in her tooth, it tasted vile, and she made the silliest of faces trying to dislodge it and complaining of the taste. It was one of those moments that isn't in the slightest bit funny to recall now, but made you laugh a lot at the time. We went off to pick Matt up and then dropped Mum off at home. I got out of the car gave her a hug, and she went down the path to her door.

The next evening I rang her for a chat, as I always spoke to her every day. She loved to tell me about the things she had watched on TV and the minute details of the plotlines. She loved murder mysteries and watched all the detective series. Often I would not be listening properly, so filled in the gaps with mm, ah, yeah, as you do when you are only half-listening. She was lonely, and my brother wasn't great company.

He spent all his time in his room, being waited on hand and foot by my poor mum, whilst chatting to his Filipino girlfriend on Skype, but he did venture out occasionally. She told me that she had a pain in the groin, but didn't say it was serious. I said she should see a doctor and she replied that if it wasn't gone by morning, she would. She was not very good at going to the doctor. They had made such huge mistakes while she was being misdiagnosed when her tummy was bad that she had little confidence in them.

Matt was at work, so after the call, I went about putting Jacob to bed and settling down to the Saturday night TV. Just before 9 pm, I got a call from my brother. He had arranged to go through to watch a film with Mum at 8.30 and just around then called through to her. "I will be through in a minute. Just going to the loo."

"OK," came the reply back. A few minutes later, he went into the living room. Mum was sat in her chair, slumped over after having a heart attack.

He carried her to the floor and rang 999. They told him what to do for CPR whilst the ambulance came. He tried his best, bearing in mind my brother is a strapping six feet, 'built like a tank' guy and my mum was a dainty little five feet, three inches in the end. It must have been so hard to try to pump on the chest of your own mum. He was a great big softy who didn't like blood or needles. He loved her so much too. He was the baby out of all her children. I cannot begin even to think of how I would have felt in those moments. It breaks my heart to write about this even twelve years later.

The ambulance arrived swiftly, as the hospital was only a mile away. The paramedics tried but failed to get her heart started again and rushed her off to hospital. That is when Ricky, my brother, rang me. I rang Matt, and he rushed home. Luckily, he worked at the local station. I quickly got dressed and saw the little jade green angel my mum had just bought me for my birthday and slipped it into my jeans pocket. I have no idea why.

We drove at breakneck speed to Newcastle, only to find she was at the local hospital around the corner from her house. In his confusion, Ricky had told me the wrong hospital, but eventually we arrived and rushed to her side. They had started her heart again with drugs, but it had taken half an hour. She was tied to monitors, with tubes everywhere and she looked as if she was gone. I could just tell, I just knew.

I sat by her side and took her hand. It was still warm, as the machines were still pumping. Then I remembered I had the angel in my pocket, so I took it and placed it in her hand, wrapping her fingers tightly around it and holding them shut, praying to the angel, all the angels, God, heaven, the Universe, anyone to help change the outcome.

The doctors came to do tests to see if her brain was active. I unfurled her fingers and took the angel, who was now warm. Leaving the room, I carried on hoping and praying, holding the little angel hand tight as I could. The doctors finished and went to write up their findings. I once again took Mum's beautiful slim, elegant hand and wrapped the angel up in her fingers again. Nobody knew I was doing this, only me.

I held tighter and tighter as the nurse came round. "I am sorry," she said, "There is no brain activity."

The time had come to switch off the machine. For the next few seconds that felt like minutes, the machine beeped then stopped, then beeped a few times, then stopped several times. At each beep, I said to her silently, "Come on, Mum...fight, please fight." The deathly silence came, and I knew for sure it was over. I unwrapped her fingers for the last time and wrapped mine around the little jade angel's body, in a manner in which it felt as if I would never let go. That little angel still goes everywhere with me. She was the last thing my mum touched, and It feels like she left a piece of herself within it. I tried my very best to be strong, but I was feeling dead inside once more. Everything went into automatic mode. I had to focus just on breathing in and breathing out.

I swore I would never step foot in my car again. I couldn't, as it would have been too painful without her sitting there.

The next morning I had to face up to the realisation that I had some decisions to make as to what to do with her body. The one thing I knew for sure was that there was no way on this earth I was going to give her one of those morose Victorian funerals with a black hearse and limousine cars, the same as just about every other person was given. As the last thing I could ever do for her, I wanted something befitting, something personal. Traditional funerals are not personal and are mostly all the same. People seem to want to do the normal thing, but in a time of grief, I suppose they want someone to make all the arrangements. They aren't thinking outside of the box. Of course, I had to work within our budget as Mum had barely two pennies left to her name. In the months before her passing, I had seen a go-as-you-please type of funeral parlour open up outside of town. I knew I couldn't lay her in a cold, dark, haunting cemetery, but neither could I watch a casket been drawn into the hellfire of an incinerator as they had done with both my nana and grandad. My nana specifically did not want to be cremated, but my aunt gave her no choice.

I rang for some advice, and the gentleman (or Earth Angel) on the other end of the phone could not have been more helpful. He explained that I could do as wished. I told him my own thoughts, and he helped me narrow things down. I could not have faced picking her up from the mortuary and dressing her, so I would need someone to do that for me and provide a parlour to keep her until the date of the burial. The gentleman agreed to do these jobs for me. I selected a wicker casket so that it was natural and beautiful, like my mum.

I decided that she should be buried in a wildflower woodland field that was just starting as a burial place, called Seven Penny Meadows. It was on a hill overlooking Newcastle/Gateshead, and the River Tyne from a distance. I did not want to take her there in a funeral car where many dead people had been before and would be after. We had a Mondeo and with the seats down her casket fitted perfectly, even with both my brother Rick and Matt's brother Aaron in the car. This was to be the last journey of my mum's body. She would have loved the idea of Matt picking her up for one last time to take her to the place of rest we had chosen for her. She loved Matt like a son, and he loved her like a mum. After all, his own had been a sorry excuse for a mum. It was an honour for Matt to drive her one last time.

In the days that proceeded, I found it so hard not being able to call her, speak to her, tell her about my day and to listen to her TV ramblings.

I felt like I needed a place to be with her. On around the third or fourth day after her passing, I decided to sit in my car, which was parked on the drive facing my garage door. It felt like the only place I could go, the last place I had seen her alive and been with her. I climbed into the driver's seat, tears rolling down my face. I just decided to start talking aloud to her. I did not know if she could hear me, but I wanted to do it anyway. Within a few minutes of starting, the front doorbell starting ringing. It rang and rang and rang. Matt rushed down to ask why I was doing that to see that I was just sitting in the car.

I looked up to the sky and just smiled. I knew exactly what it meant. You see there was something I forgot to tell you. Do you remember me telling you that the last day I saw her she had taken the bus down to my house as usual for us to go out in my car? OK, well my door was always open, so much so that even my neighbours would just walk in. Having M.E, it was always easier than getting up and going to answer the door, and I liked that people felt comfortable, that my home was inviting enough. Of course, my mum would always just walk in too. That day, the last day, she did not just come in as usual but rang the doorbell. I remember going to the door and seeing that she looked so radiant and beautiful, and I said that to her. I also asked why she had rung the bell, and she just giggled and walked in. I had not thought anymore about it until that day when the doorbell starting ringing furiously.

You see I believe she knew she was going to die, maybe not consciously but she knew. She was preparing. Funnily enough, in the months leading up to her death, she had become increasingly more spiritual. She readily absorbed all the information I was learning, all my stories of the things I had seen. She too started having her own experiences. One week, she had a very bad cold, which always went to her chest. I had been quite worried about her, so I asked my 'Gatekeeper' Vlad to go and look after her and make sure she was OK. I had no idea if this was possible, as I was still very much on the very edges of knowledge of things spiritual (as I am even to this day).

She rang me as normal the next day. Her story was that she was getting out of bed, slightly groggy, as she was on a morning, went over to open her curtains to let the daylight in, turned round and saw a figure of a man standing in her doorway. She described him to me. He was my man, my Vlad! Wow, that actually worked. I did indeed send Vlad to take care of her. He does like to stand in doorways, and it is where he is always seen.

The next day she saw him again. She accepted it and didn't question what she saw. After all, as a very sick child encased in an iron lung, she says she looked in the mirror above her and saw Jesus standing behind her. She also said she saw him once more, in my grandad's shed of all places. She said she saw the wounds in his hands from the nails. In the week running up to her passing, she had gotten out of bed on the Wednesday (she passed on the Saturday), felling still groggy as she made her way to the kitchen for her morning ritual cup of tea. Standing by the oven waiting for the little gas kettle to whistle, she glanced to her left, and there right at her shoulder was a figure. She said she jumped out of her skin and stumbled sideways, grabbing onto the kitchen bench to prevent her fall, and shouted out loud, "Bloody hell, I'm going to have a frigging heart attack!" Three days later, she did.

The day finally came. Matt, Rick and Aaron picked her up from the parlour and took her to Seven Penny Meadows where a little gazebo tent was waiting for her. I drove up with my neighbour Peter as my co-pilot. I requested that those who attended wore anything but black, and recommended they wore wellies. I only invited immediate family, and some of my friends came to support me, or those that knew my mum. I didn't want a bunch of hypocritical people, who couldn't have given a monkey about her while she was alive, suddenly turning up as if they cared. I asked for donations to Crohn's disease research instead of flowers, but made her a huge bunch of multi-coloured roses that I arranged and hand-tied myself. I thread some of the flowers through the wickerwork of the casket; some of my friends helped to do this too. It looked so pretty.

I had arranged for my brother Rick to read her favourite poem, 'Footprints in the Sand'. You know, the one where the person saw two sets of footprints in the sand all their life, and at the hardest times there was only one set. The person asks God, "Why did you abandon me at those most crucial parts of my life?" God's reply was,

"I did not abandon you at those most important times. I carried you." She loved that poem. My other brother (who had to be accompanied, as he was a patient in a lockdown mental hospital) played the music I had chosen — 'Amazing Grace', a favourite of hers. I wrote the eulogy.

After the poem and the eulogy, my two brothers, with Matt and Aaron, carried her casket to the trestle tables waiting just by the hole in the ground. They stepped back as I played Nat King Cole's 'Smile'. This was a song that expressed exactly who she was -- someone who could smile regardless of the pain she was in physically or emotionally, whose smile lit up her face and showed how beautiful she was from the very core to beyond the surface. My aunt started crying, knowing the significance of the words.

The most beautiful part was when the words, "And the sun came shining through," were sung. At that moment, a sunbeam shot through the thickly clouded sky and shone directly onto the casket. It was timed to absolute perfection, because as this golden sunbeam came down like a giant torch lighting up the pretty flowers, a little butterfly flew in and landed right there in the sunlight on the roses. Everybody took a massive gasp. They all just stopped and stared in amazement. I couldn't have asked for it to be any better, even if had got Steven Spielberg to direct it. It was almost as if she was there herself, saying, "Yes, you got it absolutely spot on and here is my contribution."

We decided after the funeral to sell the house. We wanted a fresh start and were seriously considering taking a sabbatical and living in Turkey for five years. There was nothing stopping us now. The house sold quickly, but the housing market crashed at the same time, and our buyers pulled their offer and offered a ridiculously low price. On a normal day there wouldn't have been a hope in hell's chance of selling at that price, but we were not thinking straight with grief, and we just felt the need to run away I guess, at least now looking back that is what I was doing.

Eventually, we decided not to go to Turkey, the way the climate was, and the police cutbacks. They no longer wanted to give you a job after a sabbatical. We decided to move to Durham, where we found a beautiful new house to make our own. In-between selling and moving, we already had tickets booked for Turkey well before Mum had passed, so we went to spend some time in our spiritual home, where we felt peace and serenity.

We decided to buy a swinging chair in memory of Mum, and put it on the back porch. This was Matt's favourite spot, and I know that, if she had visited there before she passed away, it would have been her favourite too. Matt spent most of the holiday on her chair. I think I cooked, cleaned and shopped for new furniture just to try not to think about what had happened.

I had only been there a few days when the weirdest thing happened. I had been sleeping in Jacob's bedroom, which was at the back. Ja was in bed with snoring Matt. I woke suddenly in the night, as I felt someone was in the room with me. I opened my eyes to see a pattern of energy forming…it formed and shaped as I watched it, and it was also moving towards me. As it began to clear, I could see the familiar features of Mum. I didn't know what to say and just lay and watched as she moved above me, floating parallel. I could see all of her so clearly. She looked so sad, and then a single tear fell from her eye. It too was made of the pure white energy, as she was. It fell towards me and dissipated.

OMG! My mind suddenly raced. She must have gone back to the other side and seen what was in store for me. This is why she was so sad! Of course, I am a great one for over-thinking. I watched as she slowly disappeared and thanked her for visiting. She had given me the doorbell signal, and now here she was actually showing me she was OK. Was she OK, though? Why was she crying? It stayed with me all of the next day.

That night I opted once again to sleep on my own in the back room, to be woken again by the same kind of event as the night before. There she was once more, my beautiful mum, radiant and youthful staring down at me, this time with a giant beaming smile across her face. She had come back to say it was OK, she was happy. I held my hand up and did a little wave to her, and a little wave of fingers came back. I felt so much peace and love. I wish she could have stayed there for longer, but she dissipated once more.

I cried myself back to sleep, as I felt so overwhelmed by emotions. There was my mum, and I could see her, I could know she was OK, but I could not give her a cuddle or talk to her. I then understood why she was crying the first night. She had been sad that she had to leave Jacob and me. She was just showing that, although I felt that she knew it was the right time for her.

While I was in Turkey, I wanted to meet up with Kim, who I had met a few years earlier. She was a medium and gave great readings. We had always met for coffee when I was out there. Kim was originally from Newcastle, so we had a bond through that. I trusted Kim. You could see the kindness in her face. She reminded me somehow of my mum, one of those people who just trust and believe in people. She oozed a calm serenity and beauty even when she was in a massive pickle inside. I figured if anyone could make me feel OK, then Kim could.

I went to her for a spiritual reading. I felt I needed that after all that had happened recently. She had given me quite an accurate reading before, so I felt I would get the same this time. We met in a cafe she liked. We didn't catch up much as she wanted to get straight into the reading. She has a little tin of shells and pebbles that she uses as a tool. She reads them first, and this helps her calm and connect with spirit.

I can't quite remember what the pebbles read, because I was so overwhelmed by what she said next. She told me she had a lady with her, and that this felt like a 'mother' energy. She said the lady was beautiful and had a smile that lit up her face, and that she was standing here right beside me beaming with pride. She said the lady apologised for having to leave, but she knew I was going to be OK as I had such amazing strength. Kim said, "OK," to the lady, then turned to me and said, "This lady tells me what she has said is not enough validation for you. She wants me to show you this…I have no idea what it means, so I am giving you exactly what she is showing me: A little green angel, and the lady keeps opening and closing her hand. She tells me that this is all you need to know to validate exactly who she is and that she is alive and well in the spirit world."

I burst out crying, with those cartoon tears that seem to squirt out of your eyes. There was no time for drops as there were too many tears. I was in utter shock at what she had said. Nobody but my dying, brain-dead mum and myself knew anything about that little green angel, or the way I had kept putting it in the palm of her hand and wrapping her fingers around it. That meant even though her body was being kept alive by machines and her brain was dead, she was still in that room. Likely, she was watching what was happening to her once her energy had left the body it once resided in.

Wow, wow, wow! In all of my few years of book reading, researching, speaking to spiritual people and seeing spirits of all kinds myself, those few words were the ultimate validation that we are energy, and life does go on beyond the physical parameters of a human body. Mum knew she had to cross over, but she did everything she could to validate to me that everything I believed in was true. She knew that it would be her last gift to me, as the beautiful burial was my last gift to her. It was her way of leaving me with something I could never forget, and which would shape my life for evermore. Kim did not know the impact those few words had on me. She was but a deliverer of the most amazing gift which shaped my life and got me through some tough times

I have lots more to write. It is now Autumn of 2020 and so much has happened, but I have to save that for another day. I want to start writing my spiritual diaries so that you can see and read all of the weird things that have happened to me. I would like to leave you with a few little thoughts that I have found have helped me through the darkest of times. I started to think this way around my mum's passing, how I looked back at it and saw how it fitted into this huge jigsaw puzzle, each piece interlinked with another. If I had not have gone to Turkey with Jacob and picked up that virus/bacterial infection, I would not have become so ill that I felt the need to start learning to drive. Had I not started to learn to drive, I would not have had those last six weeks or so with Mum, where some of the validations of her passing happened, such as ringing the doorbell, having the car as a tool to feel close to her.

I can look even further back to all the crazy ideas I had of moving abroad. If I had not have talked about it so much and had that idea so strongly in my head, I would not have driven Matt to agree to buying a house. Without that house, none of this would have happened. I can look and cross-reference so much, like how she seemed to be putting her affairs together in the weeks before she died, yet was happier and had more stability in her health than for years before. I don't believe we can know the time we will pass over, but I do believe there are several times that are put on our path when we can choose to leave.

You see, I have come to believe that we write many of our own stories before we have even taken our place inside the human body we will inhabit. I believe whatever path we take, there are lessons we give ourselves, milestones that we will reach that we cannot avoid. We have free will in all other aspects, but we will always come to these milestones, these lessons but not necessarily learn them this time around, though. It sometimes takes lifetimes with the same lessons in order to learn them. Some are difficult and can take us to the edge of our tolerance. For instance, my life has it felt at times that I have been hanging over a cliff by my fingernails.

However, we do not give ourselves more than we know our soul can cope with, although as a soul, we sometimes forget the fragility of being human. As a soul, we want to experience everything, every emotion, every feeling, no matter how good or bad it seems to us as a human. We need all sorts of different lives, short and long, rich and poor, gifted and tragic. We won't finish our soul growth until we have experienced everything possible.

You see, for me, it is a life-changer when you take responsibility for things that happen, when you do not allow anyone to make you a victim. Sometimes that statement seems unfair because we see so many bad things happening to good people. What if in their soul lives those people decided to sacrifice this lifetime to be the lesson for someone else? Are they then still a victim? I know this is big stuff, but I do know this way of thinking has helped me so much over the years.

After all, if I had not been poorly with M.E, I would not have willingly chosen to stop, give up work and let myself rest to have a baby. There was always a massive risk to my kidney. Having M.E gave me the time to do just that. Without M.E, I would not have the amazing child I have, now eighteen years old, and the finest young man you could ever wish for. He is sweet, loving and kind, polite and chivalrous to ladies, a beautiful old soul if ever there were one. His soul is even older than mine. I was told by a medium once that he chose to come to me in order to look after me, which he does so well, bless him. If it wasn't for the M.E, I would have never stopped and therefore not found my spiritual path. I would have carried on running around like a headless chicken, trying to fix everyone else's problems and not sort my own life out.

OK, I get frustrated sometimes, quite a lot of times, but I go with the flow. I sit and watch life go by, and I remain grateful that I wake every morning that every day is a new opportunity. I live with hope that one day they find the cure. I know that will happen — I have asked the Universe. I believe in that too. You are an energy, a drop of the ocean that we call the Universe. We are all the same kind of drops, none more special than the others are.

We are each a tiny piece of the entirety of everything there is. Some people call that entirety God, Allah or Buddha, a mass consciousness we return to when we have finished punishing ourselves in these fragile human bodies, an energy that we are, that we think and that we make true. I have seen so many times how powerful thoughts are, how creative they are for both good and bad.

My friends, thank you so much for reading, and I hope I have left you with a few new thoughts. Until next time, when I share my spirit diaries with you or update you with the stories of the last eight years, I hope you will find time to meet with me again on another page.

Sending love and light to you.
LOVE always,
Julia

Printed in Great Britain
by Amazon